LIBRARY 2.0 AND BEYOND

LIBRARY 2.0 AND BEYOND

Innovative Technologies and Tomorrow's User

EDITED BY NANCY COURTNEY

FOREWORD BY STEVEN J. BELL

LIBRARIES

UNLIMITED

A Member of the Greenwood Publishing Group

Westport, Connecticut • London

Library of Congress Cataloging-in-Publication Data

Library 2.0 and beyond : innovative technologies and tomorrow's user / edited by Nancy Courtney.
    p. cm.
  Includes bibliographical references and index.
  ISBN-13: 978–1–59158–537–4 (alk. paper)
  1. Libraries and the Internet.   2. Libraries–Information technology.
  I. Courtney, Nancy.   II. Title: Library two point zero and beyond.
Z674.75.I58L545   2007
020.285′4678–dc22   2007009007

British Library Cataloguing in Publication Data is available.

Library of Congress Catalog Card Number: 2007009007
ISBN-13: 978-1-59158-537-4

First published in 2007

Libraries Unlimited, 88 Post Road West, Westport, CT 06881
A Member of the Greenwood Publishing Group, Inc.
www.lu.com

Printed in the United States of America

The paper used in this book complies with the
Permanent Paper Standard issued by the National
Information Standards Organization (Z39.48–1984).

10 9 8 7 6 5 4 3 2 1

CONTENTS

PREFACE

Are you feeling more pressure at your library not only to keep up with the latest technologies, but also to implement them now because everyone else is too? All librarians must confront the technology ratchet that continually tightens its grip around library staff and their patrons. As the pace of technology change accelerates, many librarians routinely ask themselves, "how will I keep up?" What ideas and techniques do we have at our disposal to slow the pace at which the ratchet tightens so that our ability to learn and integrate new technologies into our practice is more manageable?

Realistically, we are unlikely ever to slow the pace of technology change, but our best defense in the battle to cease being overwhelmed by new technology is to proactively learn and understand what these new technologies do and how they are being used. It isn't necessary to use or gain expertise with every one of them. But it is critical to understand what the new technologies are and what results they deliver. In your hands you have a powerful tool for contributing to a personal and professional development strategy to gain a deep understanding of technology tools and applications that have real promise to improve library services. Collectively these technologies are referred to as Web 2.0. In this book, a collection of early adopters describe these technologies and share ideas for using them in library settings. While it has yet to resonate with all library practitioners, Library 2.0 offers a reasonably good term to express how Web 2.0 concepts, practices, and technologies can be integrated into the library domain. However one feels about Library 2.0, there is no denying the resources described in this book can contribute to a better library user experience. And there's also no denying that editor Nancy Courtney has assembled a stellar cast of contributors to introduce you to these technologies, and how they are being applied in libraries. What many of these authors share is a notable article or blog post that established each as a visionary thought leader to whom others looked for guidance and clear thinking on the technologies that constitute the world of Library 2.0.

Whether you've been following the Library 2.0 conversation closely or have paid it little attention, this collection has something to offer. For those new to the conversation, Elizabeth Black's chapter on Web 2.0 makes a perfect starting point because as she states, "In order to understand the concept of Library 2.0, it is important to understand what Web 2.0 is and is not." She details the origins of Web 2.0 and explains what it is through a set of principles identified by Tim O'Reilly, credited with first coining the term. Black then provides an overview of Web 2.0 tools such as blogs, wikis, and podcasts that are profiled individually in later chapters. Her chapter enters its final phase with a review of the evolution of the Library 2.0. It was a process that was not without some controversy, and this chapter concludes that whatever one thinks about Web 2.0 or Library 2.0, it's essential for libraries and those who run them to keep pace with these new technologies.

One of the most popular topics of conversation among librarian bloggers was dissatisfaction with the library catalog. Rare is the librarian for whom the phrase "the OPAC sucks" is without some meaning. How would a library catalog perform if it didn't suck? The answer to that question is what Michael Casey seeks to share with readers in the next chapter. Casey identifies himself, not as a programmer or cataloger, but simply a catalog user. From there he provides a user's perspective on how the Internet has shifted user expectations about search systems, and how that has made the OPAC's glaring design and usability faults all the more noticeable to librarians and their user communities. He then provides his vision for OPAC 2.0, and describes the many ingredients it will require. Not surprisingly a good number of these features are influenced by Internet search and retailing firms that understand how users think. But Casey reminds us there is hope. He wraps up his chapter by introducing some notable library projects designed to make the OPAC a resource that both librarians and their users will truly appreciate.

And if the mantra of the twenty-first century Library 2.0 librarian is "be where the users are," then the obvious place is in a social network. That's where most of the younger generation, the ones librarians would really like to reach, are apt to be found in the Web 2.0 world. Who makes a better guide through the world of MySpace and Facebook than Brian Mathews, an early adopter of social networking at his library, where he has experimented with it to learn more about and reach out to students attending his institution? After a brief history of the social networking concept, Mathews provides a detailed overview of the features typically found in online social networks, such as profiles, groups, friending, and messaging. But the bulk of the chapter focuses on identifying the advantages and disadvantages of social networks for librarians, and then it describes those opportunities that social networks can afford to librarians who choose to wisely integrate themselves into these places where our community members increasingly go.

One of the most impressive and talked about blog posts of 2005 demonstrated a radical approach to delivering information in blog format; it was actually closer to a research article. That would be Ellyssa Kroski's post about "A Hive Mind" at her blog Infotangle. For many librarians, it was and is their primer on tagging and folksonomies. Ellyssa brings her expertise on this topic to a discussion about how ordinary people are using a collective intelligence to organize and categorize the

Internet. Even those who read the original "Hive Mind" post will learn more from this new elaboration on Kroski's original discussion. In particular she expands on the advantages and disadvantages of tagging, possible future developments, and takes a look at how libraries are integrating tagging into their resources. Bring up allowing patrons to tag a library resource, and a librarian somewhere is bound to ask if that isn't heresy and just plain dangerous. Clearly, we can all benefit from what Kroski has to say.

And who among us couldn't benefit from improving staff communication by enabling both professionals and support workers to share information easily. Chad F. Boeninger explores that fertile territory in his chapter on wikis. Wikis, explains Boeninger, are perhaps the most versatile Library 2.0 technology because it has both an internal and external capacity to encourage peer production. Internally, a wiki can be used by reference staff, for example, to share news about new resources, student assignments, or technology updates. Externally, a wiki can be a knowledge base to which both librarians and the user community can add content. As with many of the chapters you'll be reading, Boeninger's focus is less on the nuts and bolts of the technology, and much more on the "why you should use it" and "user experience" aspects that are beneficial to both library administrators and front-line practitioners.

One of the most exciting projects to grab the attention of the library world in recent times is one that truly illustrates Web 2.0's emphasis on user participation. What speaks to a higher level of participation on the web than actually becoming part of the web itself? That's what Lori Bell, Tom Peters, and Kitty Pope discuss in their chapter on Second Life, and how librarians and libraries are becoming participants in the virtual world. Bell, Peters, and Pope explain how and why they took an interest in Second Life. Recognizing the potential for offering library services to the virtual citizens of Second Life, the coauthors enlisted real and virtual colleagues to create the Second Life Library. Whatever your level of experience is with virtual worlds, you're going to learn much more about Second Life in this chapter, and what its implications are for providing services in the Library 2.0 landscape.

In the real world perhaps the hottest technology phenomenon is the mobile or handheld device. Whether it be a mobile phone, PDA, smartphone, MP3 player, tablet PC, e-book reader, gaming device, or some mixed-use handheld, these devices are rapidly gaining ubiquity. Within the next few years they'll be used heavily for web communications and information search. In his chapter, Christopher Strauber reviews what handheld computers are, and what they can do for libraries and their user communities. After identifying the many different devices that fit into the handheld category, Strauber explores how each might fit into a Library 2.0 service delivery plan. In doing so he paints a picture of a library that communicates with users in very different ways, and that is capable of delivering both text and digital media to the handheld. Libraries, along with their content providers, will be challenged to deliver aggregator database searching to the handheld. But with handhelds it will all change rapidly, and Library 2.0 may be best prepared to deal with that change.

One technology that presents far fewer barriers to entry is the podcast. As Chris Kretz says in his chapter about podcasting, it's a technology that has "come a long way in a short time." There are many examples of how libraries can use podcasts to capture booktalks, instructional guides to resources, library news, programming by featured guest and individual librarians, and much more. Each application is based on an actual library that is already using podcasting to reach out to and involve their users. Kretz also provides a wealth of information on how to get started with podcasting. He offers everything from hardware and software requirements and options, to tips for creating good podcasts, to legal issues, to promotion and branding of podcasts. If reading this chapter inspires you to try a podcast, Kretz tells you how to get started.

Libraries have always been about sharing and telling stories. In Library 2.0 there is a new twist on this traditional role: digital storytelling. According to coauthors Karen Diaz and Anne M. Fields, a digital story is simply a story told using some combination of still and moving digital images, digital voiceover narrative, and digital music. Libraries can now mix their storytelling with social networking in order to share the stories and allow users to participate by adding their own content. Because readers are less likely to be familiar with digital storytelling than some better known Web 2.0 technologies, Diaz and Fields provide many details on the elements of a digital story and how to create one that effectively delivers a message. Both librarians and their library's users have stories to tell. Now we can create and share them across networks. With help from Diaz and Fields, we can begin to develop expertise with this technology.

Few of us would think of Pong or Pacman as part of the Web 2.0 world of technology, but gaming does play an important role in shaping Library 2.0. David Ward shares his expertise to craft a chapter that reveals the true depth of computer and web-based gaming, and how they can contribute to social and learning environments. Since many librarians are unfamiliar with gaming, Ward begins with an excellent overview of the history and growth of the gaming industry. He then explores in greater detail two specific areas of interest for Library 2.0; games as educational tools and games as guides to interface design. Both impact more significantly on how gaming can provide ways for librarians to connect more effectively with their users in the Web 2.0 world. Readers will learn that games are about more than fun, which is important, but are also a social activity through which librarians can reach a segment of users that might not otherwise use the library at all. Love it or hate it, gaming is a significant cultural force that must be recognized.

And to push your Library 2.0 frontier just a bit farther, you'll need to get in tune with mashups. Even if the sound of it makes you think it's too techy for your skill level, avoid this chapter at your own risk. Eric Schnell introduces mashups in a way that makes it fairly easy to grasp. He explains that a mashup is a new application created by combining together third-party data sources. The resulting interactive web application is often an entirely new and innovative service. Schnell's supportive examples help us understand what he means by making it clear how these applications can play a role in improving library services. There's no denying that Schnell's chapter is perhaps the most technical of the book, but as with many Library 2.0 technologies you don't need to actually learn how to create or use the technology. It is important to know what the technology is and how it works. That alone makes you better informed, and able to communicate effectively with peers about these new technologies and how they might be applied in your library. We also need to understand how our information technology colleagues use these resources, and in what ways our user communities use them and expect us to use them as well.

User expectations, to my way of thinking, are why this collection of articles is so important for the library community right now. Our users dwell in a Web 2.0 world, and it shapes their interaction with information technology. It is up to library professionals to understand these technologies, and determine which can best contribute to a better library user experience in each of our libraries. We need to give our library users an opportunity to participate in the production of content for our information resources and our websites. We need to find ways to allow our library users to tell and share their stories. After all, we can try to tell our user communities about all the wonderful ways in which we can help them, but if they hear it from their peers it has the potential to deliver a much more powerful message.

Of course, learning new technology means change, and building one's comfort level with the Library 2.0 world will require some significant change and learning. Change, unfortunately, is something we often resist. But what is the alternative to learning new skills and changing? That would be marginalization and eventual obsolescence. Those are the outcomes we need to avoid, and one path is to truly understand what Library 2.0 and beyond is all about. In framing how we must cope with change I am preferential to a quote from David Bishop. In 2006 Bishop retired as University Librarian at Northwestern University after 40 years in the profession. In summing up the change he'd seen in his career he said, "We have watched whole professions go out of business as a result of changes in technology. Libraries are not immune. Change must happen soon and across the board if libraries of all types are to remain viable." He sounds like the type of library leader who would encourage others to read this book.

Steven J. Bell
Associate University Librarian for Research and Instruction Services
Temple University

1

⚊•❖•⚊

WEB 2.0 AND LIBRARY 2.0: WHAT LIBRARIANS NEED TO KNOW

Elizabeth L. Black

The term Library 2.0 first appeared in September 2005 in a post by Michael Casey in his *LibraryCrunch* blog. Library 2.0 alludes to the term Web 2.0 in an attempt to associate libraries more directly with the characteristics and technologies of Web 2.0. Soon, the term was the focus of great debate and conversation on blogs, e-mail lists, and in person among librarians and those in the library field. The quick rise of the term Library 2.0 and its forerunner, Web 2.0, shows the impact of the changes the World Wide Web have made to the way people communicate and collaborate, the very trends the terms attempt to describe. The hallmarks of Library 2.0 and Web 2.0 are that more people share their ideas, contribute content, and have easier access to collaborative tools. This chapter will describe the concepts of Library 2.0 and Web 2.0.

WEB 2.0

In order to understand the concept of Library 2.0, it is important to understand what Web 2.0 is and is not. Web 2.0 is not related to Internet2, a not-for-profit consortium that develops and deploys advanced network technologies for research and higher education (Internet2 2006). It is not a new standard or version of the Internet. It is not a specification with which an application or system must be compatible. Instead, Web 2.0 is an attempt to conceptualize the dramatic changes the web has brought to society.

O'Reilly's Definition

The term Web 2.0 is credited to Tim O'Reilly, sometimes with Dale Dougherty (*Economist* 2006) and sometimes with John Battelle (Notess 2006). It was originally coined in 2003 and was used for the conference by the same name first held in 2004 and sponsored by O'Reilly Media. Tim O'Reilly (2005b) posted this widely cited definition of the term on the *O'Reilly Radar* blog:

Web 2.0 is the network as platform, spanning all connected devices; Web 2.0 applications are those that make the most of the intrinsic advantages of that platform: delivering software as a continually-updated service that gets better the more people use it, consuming and remixing data from multiple sources, including individual users, while providing their own data and services in a form that allows remixing by others, creating network effects through an 'architecture of participation,' and going beyond the page metaphor of Web 1.0 to deliver rich user experiences.

O'Reilly first offered an expanded definition in an essay for the 2005 Web 2.0 (O'Reilly 2005a) conference. He describes Web 2.0 as a set of seven principles and practices that serve as a gravitational core. The first principle is "the web is a platform," meaning that computer programs are delivered and used over the web. Applications run inside a web browser; they do not require that the programs run on individual computers. Another element of the principle of web as platform is the idea that the software is a service. Using Google as an example, O'Reilly points out that the real commodity Google is offering is not the actual software but the information it provides to users.

O'Reilly's second principle of Web 2.0 is "harnessing collective intelligence." Another way this concept is frequently regarded is as the "wisdom of crowds." With many people contributing a small amount, the results are impressive. eBay provides a good example; its strength resides in the collective offerings of its members. In addition, eBay's competitive advantage comes from its sheer mass of buyers and sellers. Other Web 2.0 sites such as wikis, del.icio.us, and Flickr demonstrate this principle. They will be discussed in greater depth later in this book.

The third principle O'Reilly described is "data is the next *Intel inside*." He writes "every significant Internet application to date has been backed by a specialized database: Google's web crawl, Yahoo!'s directory (and web crawl), Amazon.com's database of products, eBay's database of products and sellers, MapQuest's map databases, Napster's distributed song database" (O'Reilly 2005a). These companies use their databases to provide valuable services to web users. They continually enhance their data, such as Amazon.com adding book cover images and tables of contents to the ISBN registry database they purchased from Bowker. These companies also recognize that users generate data by their use of the web. Web 2.0 companies gather this data and use it to enhance the user experience further. Look at Amazon.com; this company takes data from sales and page views and uses it to provide recommendations to other users.

The "end of the software release cycle" is O'Reilly's fourth principle. Because the business of Web 2.0 companies is to provide a service, not software, it is not important to track the software release dates and versions. These companies continually update the software they use to deliver their service. They do no wait for several changes in the software before they release another version. In fact, they view their users as extensions of the development team. The programmers regularly put out new features and evaluate how web users make use of them. If the new features get a lot of use, they are offered more broadly; if they get little use, the new features are pulled for revision or discarded altogether.

The fifth principle identified by O'Reilly is the "lightweight programming model". Simple standards that allow loose combinations of systems are the most successful. O'Reilly points to Really Simple Syndication (RSS) as a good example because of its simplicity and wide adoption. RSS will be discussed in more detail later in this chapter. Syndication is about sending information out in an easy-to-access format and not attempting to control what happens at the other end. This makes it easy for others to remix the code and content into new creations, often called mashups. Mashups will be covered in greater depth by Eric Schnell in a later chapter.

"Software above the level of a single device" is the sixth principle of Web 2.0 defined by O'Reilly. This is software that bridges the gap between the computer and other devices; it facilitates the use of the other device. A good example is iTunes; this software and website connects the iPod MP3 music player to a huge warehouse of music and expedites the transfer of files between the two.

The seventh and last principle is "rich user experiences"; it's the thing that draws users back again and again. Techniques such as Ajax made it possible to offer full applications, such as G-mail, over the web. Ajax stands for Asynchronous JavaScript and XML and is not technically a technology by itself, but is a method for combining several technologies to create a web-based experience that acts more like traditional desktop applications (Clyman 2005). Ajax does this by transferring pieces of data in the background to update part of a web page without requiring that the entire web page be reloaded. This makes more interactive experiences possible.

Other Views of Web 2.0

The concept and name of Web 2.0, however, elicits debate. Tim Berners-Lee (2006), the inventor of the World Wide Web, disagrees with the term Web 2.0. In a recent interview, he said

Web 1.0 was all about connecting people. It was an interactive space, and I think Web 2.0 is of course a piece of jargon, nobody even knows what it means. If Web 2.0 for you is blogs and wikis, then that is people to people. But that was what the Web was supposed to be all along. [...] The idea of the Web as interaction between people is really what the Web is. That was what it was designed to be as a collaborative space where people can interact.

Berners-Lee described his delight in seeing the web being used as a platform to create tools as he used the Internet to create the web. He also noted that the web as we know it now is still evolving and no one can predict what it might become in the future. The current emphasis on collaboration and the power of the collective intelligence, though, is all part of Berners-Lee's original vision. He even noted that the first browser was designed to allow editing in hypertext, not just viewing of the content. He still doesn't understand why it didn't take off when it was originally launched.

John Dvorak (2006), a well-known columnist for *PC Magazine*, also questions the Web 2.0 label. He argues that the real trend is self-service. People are using the web to do things for themselves, as they have from the beginning of the Internet. Dvorak argues that we are seeing an evolution, not a revolution. The tools that allow people to do things for themselves are simply getting more efficient. The Web 2.0 products, such as podcasts and blogs, are all built on technology from the 1990s.

Other descriptions of Web 2.0 focus on specific aspects. Robin Peek (2005, 17) says "Web 2.0 is driven by publishing content, not building pages or sites." Those who are not part of the publishing industry are now also generating a large amount of web content. Peek uses the term social publishing to describe this change. The general public can now successfully publish content without the assistance of publishing professionals using tools like blogs and wikis as well as with sites such as eBay, Monster.com, and Amazon.com.

Bryan Alexander (2006) labels contributions to large sites like Amazon.com and Wikipedia microcontent. The bar is lower for the average user to contribute to these sites because they do not need to write the entire site, just one small part of it. Together, these pieces of microcontent result in powerful websites. Customers rely on microcontent, such as reviews, written by fellow consumers. "According to Intelliseek, consumers today are 50 percent more likely to be influenced by content posted by other customers and individuals than by traditional advertising" (Holtz 2006).

Alexander (2006) emphasizes collaboration and openness in his discussion of Web 2.0. He describes the user as playing a fundamental role in the information architecture of many sites today. The success of Web 2.0 depends on two-way flow between people and organizations.

Increased Participation

When approaching the idea of Web 2.0, The Pew Internet and American Life Project started by looking at the data they had collected over the years of the project (Madden and Fox 2006). They found that the number of adults taking part in content creation and interaction activities on the web has increased. For example, in 2001 20 percent of Internet users used an online service to develop or display their photographs (Madden and Fox 2006, 2–3). In 2005, 34 percent of Internet users reported doing so. But other more traditional Internet uses have remained steady. E-mail exchange remains the most frequently reported Internet activity: 53 percent of adults in December 2005 read or sent e-mail on a typical day compared with 52 percent of adults reporting the same in 2000 (Madden and Fox 2006, 5).

No matter what the debate about the term Web 2.0, the fact is there are now more people on the web than in previous years. According to a Pew Internet and American Life Project survey completed in April 2006 (Madden 2006), 73 percent of American adults use the Internet up from 66 percent in the January 2005 survey. Many of these people are creating their own content and are active participants in their web experiences. They are no longer just reading static websites written by a few people. A summary of recent trends (Internet and American Life Project 2006), reports that 30 percent of Internet users rated a product or service, 24 percent participated in an online auction, and 19 percent said they created content of some kind for delivery via the Internet.

The increased participation of users on the web has changed the way we as a society communicate. As Shell Holtz (2006) notes, the "Internet's real significance was its promise to democratize communication." One force in making this change to greater user participation is the open source software movement. The movement can be traced back to the beginnings of the Internet when it was primarily used at universities for research (UNESCO 2006). The name Open Source came into use in 1998 following the release of the Netscape code (Open Source Initiative 2006). The programmers who collaborated with one another on their own, freely sharing their work on the newly released code, used the name Open Source to describe their unusual openness at the time of tight control of software development by companies. The ability to communicate and share work made possible by the Internet broadened the options for people with shared interests and passions to work together in a creative way (Coffin 2006). Today the open source community is strong. There are over 133,000 projects and 1,000,000 registered users of SourceForge.net, the largest repository of open source code (SourceForge.net 2006). It is significant that many of the software tools most widely described as Web 2.0 tools, such as wikis and blogs, are often open source software applications freely available to all and continually being improved upon by the Internet community at large.

Generations and Web 2.0

Generational issues play a big role in web use. For the generation that grew up with the Internet, social networking is natural, not the dramatic culture change those in previous generations find it to be. Stephen Abram and Judy Luther (2004) describe the Millennials, those born between 1982 and 2002, as being "born with the chip." These young people have grown up with computers and don't think of them as technology. Computers and devices of all sorts are part of their daily life. They are format agnostic; they are more concerned with finding the information and are unconcerned by the format. This generation is also known to be nomadic and multitaskers. The web is available 24/7 and they expect to be able to use it whenever they need to on whatever device they have available to them. Millennials are also a collaborative group. They prefer to work together and doing so on the web with tools like instant messaging (IM), blogs, and wikis is only natural. Millennials were early and heavy adopters of IM and blogs. According to a Pew Internet and American Life data memo, Internet users age 18–28 are significantly more likely to send and receive instant messages and to write blogs than older Internet users (Fox and Madden 2005).

Lee Rainie (2006) calls the Millennial generation digital natives. He describes six realities of life for digital natives that fit nicely with the concepts of Web 2.0. The first is that media and gadgets are common throughout everyday life. The second reality is that the digital natives enjoy media and carry on communications anywhere they wish with the new gadgets available to them. The members of this generation are more likely than older Americans to own laptops, MP3 players, and cell phones. The third reality is that the Internet is at the center of these changes. The Internet and the web are ubiquitous. Broadband access in homes has increased each year Pew has tracked it. Broadband Internet permits easy and fast access. The fourth reality is that multitasking is a way of life. Looking at the computer screen of a Millennial one most likely finds several IM conversations taking place at the same time the user is searching for information on web pages and listening to music (Abrams and Luther 2004). Rainie's (2006) fifth reality is that an ordinary citizen has a greater opportunity to be a publisher, moviemaker, artist, song creator, and storyteller. Rainie reports that 33 percent of online teens share their own creations online. The sixth reality is that everything will change even more in coming years. Computing power, communication power, and storage power continue to double in capacity at extraordinary rates; Moore's Law predicts doubling of computing power every 18 months, the disk law predicts the doubling of storage every 12 months, and Gilder's law predicts the doubling of communication power every 2–3 years.

Sally McMillan and Margaret Morrison (2006) sought to explore how the Internet has become an integral part of the lives of young people in a qualitative way. They found that young people reported using the Internet to meet their objectives and to remain connected to their families and friends. The virtual communities they formed supported their physical communities; specifically, the Internet was used to stay in touch with family and friends far away and to make arrangements for events locally. The young people in the study reported that they depended on the Internet to help them define themselves and to maintain social interactions. Furthermore, their peers expected a connection to the Internet and if they weren't connected, it would be more difficult to participate. McMillan and Morrison report that the participants anticipate that their dependence on the Internet will increase.

To the digital natives, or Millennials, Web 2.0 is not a change. It is the expected way of being. This large generation, almost as large as the Baby Boom generation (Abram and Luther 2004), expects libraries and other institutions to support and facilitate their use of these technologies. They are direct in their expression of these needs; for example, they will ask for assistance when they need it and will express their dissatisfaction if they consider a service to be unacceptable (Abram and Luther 2004).

WEB 2.0 TOOLS

The principles and concepts of Web 2.0 are demonstrated in the tools associated with the term. These tools facilitate collaboration and social connections, they replace desktop applications to make the web the platform, and they provide rich user experiences running regularly updated programming that uses data as a key component. Each of the tools described below meets some or all of the principles described by Tim O'Reilly and the other authors cited above.

One tool that has gotten substantial coverage at library conferences is the blog. Blog, short for weblog, is "a web site that contains an online personal journal with reflections, comments, and often hyperlinks provided by the writer" (Merriam Webster 2006). Blogs use the web as a platform. To blog, the prospective author needs to subscribe to an account with a blog provider, such as Blogspot (www.blogspot.com) or Wordpress (www.wordpress.com). A subscription includes a graphical user interface containing a simple word processor. Blogs are user friendly, thus lowering the cost of participation. They make it easy for the reader to move from reading web pages to creating their own web content.

The blog tool has moved beyond its beginnings as a personal journal. It is a powerful tool for communicating timely information. There are many blogs today associated with libraries or about library issues. Some libraries use blogs to connect with their patrons. The arrangement of content by date makes the blog an excellent tool for sharing news and event information. The Ann Arbor (MI) District Public Library website contains several blogs through which the library administration and personnel communicate with their patrons. The library welcomes comments from registered patrons on the blog. The response has been exceptionally positive (Stephens 2006).

There are also many blogs written by individuals interested in library topics. Current topics of the day are discussed and scholarly ideas are tested on these blogs. As noted previously, the term Library 2.0 debuted in a post on the *LibraryCrunch* blog by Michael Casey (2006). While blogs are primarily written by single authors, the comments feature encourages conversations between blog authors and readers. Blog authors, known as bloggers, often link back to other blogs as another way to facilitate conversations.

Most blogging software uses a system called RSS, which stands for Really Simple Syndication or Rich Site Summary, to deliver updates to readers. RSS is an XML-based format for distributing content from news and news-like websites. The news feeds usually include a headline, a brief summary of the full article or post, and a link to the item. RSS makes it possible to send content from one web page to another. The tool that pulls all of the content together is called an aggregator. There are two general types of aggregators, desktop applications or web-based applications. The benefit to using an aggregator is that the software tracks when a page has been updated and puts that content in one place to be checked. The user doesn't need to check multiple blogs or web pages regularly for new information. RSS has uses beyond blogs. The *RSS Specifications Website* (http://www.rss-specifications.com/rss-uses.htm) includes a long list of suggested uses, such as listings of real estate and other items for sale, school or business announcements, and airline flight delays.

The tools for creating multimedia content are also getting easier to use. Due to the increased ease of use, more and more people are choosing to create videos, audio files, and digital photos. The natural reaction is to want to share their creations with others. Several websites facilitate this sharing. Flickr focuses on sharing photos, YouTube provides an easy way to share video files, and iTunes facilitates the sharing of audio and video files delivered via RSS.

Collaborative writing is a hallmark of Web 2.0. Wikis are a key tool for creating written documentation by multiple authors. The first wiki was created by Ward Cunningham in 1995 in order to facilitate the sharing of programming influences with other programmers (Cunningham 1995). He called it the WikiWikiWeb (http://c2.com/cgi/wiki?WikiWikiWeb) after a shuttle bus at the Honolulu International Airport. The word wiki means "quick" in Hawaiian.

A wiki, depending on how it is set up by the administrators, allows editing by anyone or only by those with accounts. The wiki software tracks changes to all pages making the document's creation transparent to all users. Wikis are good for general content generation by many authors. This content is open to all viewers. The most famous wiki is Wikipedia, the free encyclopedia that anyone can edit. While it is controversial as an authoritative reference source, it is a remarkable success in terms of sheer amount of content available. There are 1.4 million articles in English and 2.6 million registered user accounts (Wikipedia 2006). The power of the great numbers of contributors keeps Wikipedia very current. New developments in all fields are more quickly reflected in Wikipedia than in any print encyclopedia. Likewise, errors are quickly fixed. As Chris Anderson (2006) notes, a 2005 *Nature* study found that in an analysis of forty-two entries on science topics, Wikipedia had an average of four errors per entry to the three errors per entry found in *Britannica*. Shortly after the report, the errors in

Wikipedia were corrected. So, although Wikipedia cannot be considered authoritative on an article-by-article basis, on a big-picture scale, it works. The reason is the same as that which makes the economy work; they are probabilistic systems and as such are optimized to excel over time and large numbers (Anderson 2006).

Authors who wish to collaborate but who also want to keep their work closed or those who wish to work in a graphical user interface on the web have other options available to them. Google Docs and Spreadsheets, part of which was formerly known as Writely, serves this need. As other Web 2.0 tools, Google Docs and Spreadsheets requires only a web browser and Internet access. This permits access from multiple computers and locations. Users can upload files created in other applications, create new files online, and when necessary download the files in the formats of many popular desktop word processing and spreadsheet applications. Authors collaborate by inviting others to view and edit their files. More than one person can edit a single file at a time.

Early browsers provided users with a way to get back to web pages they liked by saving the URL in a special area called bookmarks or favorites. This worked well when one person used a single computer to access the Internet. As the Internet became readily available in more places, people began using multiple computers to access the Internet. Suddenly, these bookmark and favorite files weren't sufficient. Joshua Schachter created del.icio.us in 2003 as a hobby and an informal way to tag and share web pages between friends (del.icio.us 2006). This tool uses the web as the platform; the user uses the tool through a web browser from any computer on the Internet. For each website a user saves, the person notes the title of the site, the URL (web address), and words, called tags, to describe the site.

Another key feature of del.icio.us is the sharing of the tags. When a user adds a site to their del.icio.us list, the tags assigned by other users who saved this site are displayed near the list of tags assigned to other sites by this user. Users can also see what other sites other users have tagged with specific words. This facilitates shared discovery and new ways of understanding the same content.

The University of Pennsylvania's library saw such value in social bookmarking that they created their own system. PennTags (http://tags.library.upenn.edu) is open to the entire campus community. Like most social bookmarking tools, PennTags provides access to subscribers' bookmarks from any web browser and shares the tags with all members of the community. They also offer an RSS feed for tags of the user's choice so they will be notified when anyone uses that tag.

Other websites offer tagging of their content. A notable one is Flickr. The assignment of keywords to photographs has always been challenging. The same photo elicits different reactions and means different things to different people. Tagging by many people allows for these differences. In the networked environment there is room for many ways of describing a single photo by multiple people.

The compilation of these tags forms a vibrant, living taxonomy known as folksonomy. Librarians are very familiar with taxonomy and description. These are hallmarks of the librarian profession and the entry of end users into this process is controversial among librarians. Laura Gordon-Murnane (2006) argues that folksonomies complement the use of more standard controlled vocabularies. User-generated metadata captures the rapid changes in terminology and keeps up with trends and fads. The traditional classification systems have synonym control and hierarchies to demonstrate relationships between terms. Both have valuable things to offer. The key is to find a way to use these systems together.

The Internet has become such an integral part of people's lives, it is often where they go to connect with others. This phenomenon is regularly known as social networking. The most popular sites in this area are MySpace (http://www.myspace.com/) and FaceBook (http://www.facebook.com/). MySpace is one of the most popular sites on the web with more page views than any other site on the web, except for Yahoo! (Rosenbush 2006). MySpace gives registered users a web page to personalize as they choose, within limits. There are spaces on each person's page to link to other friends on MySpace, leave messages, describe themselves, and post pictures. MySpace enhances the social aspect by making it easy to find other people with shared interests. Some suggest that it is the freedom of expression given to MySpace members that is the key to its success. Recently, it was (Garrett 2006) noted that MySpace was late to the market of social networking websites at a time when some were calling the category dead. But MySpace quickly became an integral part of the daily life of its initially mostly teenage users, adding 150,000 new users each day. Recently, MySpace has attracted an older audience. ComScore (2006) noted a significant shift in the results of an August 2006 survey that showed 40.5 percent of the MySpace user base belonging to the 35–54 age group.

FaceBook has avoided much of the problems of MySpace because it focuses on specific communities, such as universities, workplaces, and schools. In order to register with FaceBook an individual must have an e-mail address connected to one of the selected communities or domains. Access to each community is limited to its members. FaceBook also offers the option to create and join groups.

LibraryThing (http://www.librarything.com) facilitates connections among people through their personal libraries. This website assists users in cataloging their book collections by connecting them to information in known bibliographic sources and offers a tagging feature to add descriptors to the books. Users can open their collections to others, thus helping readers find other books of interest.

Mashups are often the products pointed to when describing O'Reilly's previously discussed principle, the lightweight programming model. A mashup is a website that combines data or technology from two or more sources into a single user experience. An example of a library science-related mashup is the Audience Level application OCLC research created and added to an Amazon.com record display with the use of a script in the Firefox browser (Dempsey 2006a). This application takes the ISBN from Amazon.com to identify the item in the WorldCat database. Then through an analysis of the ownership of that item by types of libraries, such as school, public, or university libraries, it determines an audience level score for the item. The score is then sent to the browser and added to the Amazon.com description of the book in question. The exciting thing about mashups, such as this one, is that the data held by long-standing library databases is now made available in new, beneficial ways.

A frequent focus of mashups is Google Maps. Creative developers often use the Google Maps interface to deliver geographical data from other sources. Darlene Fichter (2006) points to several, including Libraries411 (http://www.libraries411.com/) that offers a public library directory in map form and Weather Bonk (http://www.weatherbonk.com/) that combines weather forecasts, web cams, and maps. She shares basic directions for getting started using Google Maps to create a mashup.

LIBRARY 2.0

Library 2.0, the term, was first used widely by Michael Casey (2005) and Ken Chad and Paul Miller (2005). Both were attempting to apply Web 2.0 ideas to libraries. Michael Casey, with Laura Savastinuk (2006), defined Library 2.0 as

A model for library service that encourages constant and purposeful change, inviting user participation in the creation of both the physical and the virtual services they want, supported by consistently evaluating services. It also attempts to reach new users and better serve current ones through improved customer-driven offerings. Each component by itself is a step toward better servicing our users; however, it is through the combined implementation of all of these that we can reach Library 2.0.

Casey and Savastinuk's definition does not require Web 2.0 technologies; however they note that these technologies play a significant role in a library's ability to keep up with the changing needs of its users.

Chad and Miller (2005) were also early to define the term Library 2.0. They offered four principles for their definition. The first principle is "the library is everywhere." "Library 2.0 is available at the point of need, visible on a wide range of devices, and integrated with services from beyond the library" (Chad and Miller 2005, 9). "The library has no barriers" is their second principle. They argue that libraries should be at the heart of the democratization of information by making it easier for the general public to access and participate in the generation of the actual content. The third principle is "the library invites participation" from library staff, technology partners, and the wider community. Chad and Miller's fourth principle is "the library uses flexible best-of-breed systems" built on a new relationship between libraries and a range of technology partners. The components of the system are purchased by different vendors and mixed together for the benefit of all; the days of a single Integrated Library System (ILS) provider are numbered.

Jack Maness (2006) proposes a third definition of Library 2.0: "the application of interactive, collaborative, and multi-media Web-based technologies to Web-based library services and collections." Maness breaks his theory down into four essential elements: (1) it is user centered, (2) it provides a multimedia experience, (3) it is socially rich, and (4) it is communally innovative.

Maness argues that the library catalog must change as libraries embrace Library 2.0. As the profession moves from one that is focused on creating systems controlled by librarians and simply searched by patrons, librarians must create mechanisms for patrons to create their own systems and to contribute content to our systems. The result, when viewed through the catalog, will be a catalog of both reliable and less reliable, or suspect, holdings that include web pages, blogs, wikis, and other newer content dissemination tools. For a further discussion on the library catalog of the future, see Michael Casey's chapter.

Library 2.0 is not without its detractors. T. Scott Plutchak (2006a) argues that the term Library 2.0 is meaningless because the term suggests that the changes in libraries are radical, when they are actually evolutionary. Librarians in the past have sought out the newest technologies and sought to provide good customer service. Plutchak (2006b) notes that libraries have evolved many times as the communities they serve have changed. When librarians embrace the changes in technology and society to find new and more effective ways to serve their patrons, they are not acting in brand-new 2.0 ways, they are simply being good librarians.

Marshall Breeding (2006) argues that many libraries have yet to reach Web 1.0. In a recent review of library websites, he found that a large number of libraries either have no website at all or have sites that are seriously outdated. The number of major library websites that failed to follow web development and accessibility standards especially surprised him. As libraries move toward the more strict standards-based technologies associated with Web 2.0, he notes that they must improve their technical practices.

Talis, a United Kingdom-based ILS company, held a series of discussions with both proponents and critics of the term and concepts of Library 2.0, which they delivered as podcasts (http://talk.talis.com/). The participants engaged in a lively debate about the meaning of the term and other related issues, such as mashups and folksonomies.

Walt Crawford (2006), in an attempt to gain understanding of Library 2.0, devoted an entire issue of *Cites & Insights*, an online library science serial, to the topic. He provides sixty-two views and seven definitions of Library 2.0 with a prologue and epilogue of his own writing. Crawford quotes extensively from the many authors of web content in all its forms on the topic. The issue provides a summary of the many perspectives. Crawford notes the distinction between the concept of Library 2.0 and the bandwagon called "Library 2.0." He concludes that most of the ideas behind the concept Library 2.0 are constructive and lead to improvements in library services as they inspire experiments in libraries across the country. Fitting into this category are the discussions about focusing on the user and continuous improvement. The "Library 2.0" bandwagon, on the other hand, he argues, is simply hype and actually detracts from the ideas in the concept by its confrontational tone and negative assertions about existing libraries. The bandwagon proclaims revolution and the necessity of focusing exclusively on new technologies to save libraries. Crawford concludes that innovative librarians will experiment with the initiatives of Library 2.0 within the context of successful existing services and that some will be successful. These successes will be evolutionary, however, not revolutionary.

BEYOND COMPUTERS

The changes inspired by Web 2.0 go beyond the use of computers. They can be felt in politics, in business markets, and in society in general. New ways of communicating and sharing information over the web are increasingly becoming integrated into everyday life.

Americans are turning to the Internet for their political news and information in greater numbers. In August 2006, 26 million Americans sought news or information about the upcoming mid-term elections on the Internet (Horrigan 2006). This was a record high; it was even greater than the 21 million Americans who, according to a Pew survey conducted in November 2004, used the Internet for political information during the last presidential election. The increase is significant because mid-term elections usually draw less interest than presidential ones and because the survey was conducted in August, earlier in the election season than the 2004 survey. Horrigan suggests that this increase in usage is explained in part by the increase in engaging political content on the web from established news organizations, campaigns, independent media, and interested citizens.

The impact of Web 2.0 has changed the retail business significantly, as Chris Anderson (2004, 2006), editor-in-chief of *Wired* magazine, explains in his theory called the Long Tail. Anderson argues that the future of retail and entertainment, and potentially many other business enterprises, is in niche markets, not hits or best sellers. The Internet, with its networking connections of people and information, provides virtually unlimited selection, allowing the restrictions of limited shelf space in physical retailers to be overcome. The Long Tail depends on Web 2.0 because it is the consumers themselves who make the connections to the niches from the hits by writing reviews and recommendations and ranking products. O'Reilly's second principle of Web 2.0, harvesting the collective intelligence, is a key component of the Long Tail.

Lorcan Dempsey (2006b), Vice President, Research, and Chief Strategist at OCLC, analyzed the Long Tail concept applied to libraries. He found that libraries have collectively managed the long tail of research, learning, and cultural materials; however, the transaction costs, the costs users incur as they use the library supply system, are high. Dempsey concludes that libraries should seek unification of the discovery experience, project library discovery options into other environments, such as search engines, utilize registries of the holdings of multiple libraries more effectively, and explore ways to aggregate demand.

The ubiquitous nature of the web in current society is having an impact on the culture. "Virtual third places" (Soukup 2006) are increasingly taking the place of physical third places, those places that people frequent that are outside of the home and work environments. Dire predictions were made about the lack of third places in American society due to the suburban infrastructure, demanding work roles, and consumer lifestyles. While Soukup (2006) notes that virtual third places do not fulfill all of the needs of physical third places, they can provide a means to create new virtual places that offer similar forms of localized informal interaction and community building.

Libraries and librarians continue to evolve in response to the culture and communities around them. The world is changing at a rapid pace. In order to remain relevant to their communities, libraries must keep pace. Web 2.0 and Library 2.0 are simply attempts to describe the changes the web has brought to society. The increased participation and collaboration in the creation of web content and tools is full of potential for libraries and librarians. As Mary Ellen Bates (2006) notes, librarians have always been cutting edge and still are on the forefront of implementing and experimenting with Web 2.0 tools. The key is to continue to do so.

REFERENCES

Abram, Stephen and Judy Luther. "Born with the chip." *Library Journal* 129, no. 8 (2004): 34–37.

Alexander, Bryan. "A New Wave of Innovation for Teaching and Learning?" *Educause Review* 41, no. 2 (2006): 32–44.

Anderson, Chris. *The long tail: Why the future of business is selling less of more.* New York: Hyperion, 2006.

———. "The long tail." *Wired Magazine,* no. 12.10 (October 2004). http://www.wired.com/wired/archive/12.10/tail.html.

Bates, Mary Ellen. "Cutting edge or over the edge?" *Econtent* 29, no. 5 (2006): 31.

Berners-Lee, Tim. "Interview by Scott Laningham." *IBM DeveloperWorks.* IBM, August 22, 2006. http://www-128.ibm.com/developerworks/podcast/dwi/cm-int082206.html.

Breeding, Marshall. "Web 2.0? Let's get to Web 1.0 first." *Computers in Libraries* 26, no. 5 (2006): 30–33.

Casey, Michael. "Library 2.0—Like it or hate it, it's public domain." [weblog entry] *LibraryCrunch,* May 26, 2006. http://www.librarycrunch.com/2006/05/library_20_like_it_or_hate_it.html.

Casey, Michael and Laura C. Savastinuk. "Library 2.0." *Library Journal* 131, no. 14 (2006): 40–42.

Chad, Ken and Paul Miller. *Do libraries matter? The rise of Library 2.0.* Birmingham, UK: Talis, 2005. http://www.talis.com/downloads/white_papers/DoLibrariesMatter.pdf.

Coffin, Jill. "Analysis of open source principles in diverse collaborative communities." *First Monday* 11, no. 6 (2006). http://www.firstmonday.org/issues/issue11_6/coffin/index.html.

ComScore Networks. "More than half of MySpace visitors are now age 35 or older, as the site's demographic composition continues to shift." *Measuring the Digital Age, Press Releases,* 2006. http://www.comscore.com/press/release.asp?press=1019 (accessed November 15, 2006).

Clyman, John. "Better web-app interfaces with AJAX." *PC Magazine* 24, no. 23 (2005): 76.

Crawford, Walt. "Library 2.0 and 'Library 2.0'." *Cites & Insights: Crawford at Large* 6, no. 2 (2006). http://cites.boisestate.edu/civ6i2.pdf (accessed November 6, 2006).

Cunningham, Ward. "Invitation to the patterns list." *WikiWikiWeb,* 1995. http://c2.com/cgi/wiki?InvitationToThePatternsList (accessed November 6, 2006).

Del.icio.us. "Everything else to know about del.icio.us." http://del.icio.us/help/team (accessed November 13, 2006).

Dempsey, Lorcan. "Structured data, Web 2.0 libraries." Presentation given at 21st Annual Computers in Libraries Conference, March 22–24, 2006a, in Washington, DC. http://www.oclc.org/research/presentations/dempsey/cil2006.ppt.

———. "Libraries and the long tail: Some thoughts about libraries in a network age." *D-Lib Magazine* 12, no. 4 (2006b). http://www.dlib.org/dlib/april06/dempsey/04dempsey.html.

Dvorak, John. "Web 2.0 Baloney." *PC Magazine* 25, no. 5 (2006): 61.

Economist. "The enzyme that won." *Economist* 379, no. 8477 (2006): 80.

Fichter, Darlene. "Doing the monster mashup." *Online* 30, no. 4 (2006): 48–50.

Fox, Susannah and Mary Madden. *Generations Online.* Washington, DC: Pew Internet and American Life Project, 2005. http://www.pewinternet.org/PPF/r/170/report_display.asp (accessed November 12, 2006).

Garrett, Jessie James. "MySpace: Design anarchy that works." *Business Week Online,* January 3, 2006. http://www.businessweek.com/innovate/content/dec2005/id20051230_570094.htm.

Gordon-Murnane, Laura. "Social bookmarking, folksonomies, and Web 2.0 tools." *Searcher* 14, no. 6 (2006): 26–38.

Holtz, Shell. "Communicating in the world of Web 2.0." *Communication World* 23, no. 3 (2006): 24–27.

Horrigan, John B. *Politics Online*. Pew Internet and American Life Data Memo, 2006. http://www.pewinternet.org/PPF/r/187/report_display.asp (accessed November 8, 2006).

Internet and American Life Project. "Internet Activities." *Latest Trends*, 2006. http://www.pewinternet.org/trends/Internet_Activities_7.19.06.htm (accessed November 8, 2006).

Internet2's official website. Home page http://www.internet2.edu/ (accessed November 8, 2006).

Madden, Mary. *Internet penetration and impact*. Washington, DC: Pew Internet and American Life Project, 2006. http://www.pewinternet.org/PPF/r/182/report_display.asp.

Madden, Mary and Susannah Fox. *Riding the waves of "web 2.0": More than a buzzword, but still not easily defined*. Washington, DC: Pew Internet and American Life Project, 2006. http://www.pewinternet.org/PPF/r/189/report_display.asp.

Maness, Jack M. "Library 2.0 theory: Web 2.0 and its implications for libraries." *Webology* 3, no. 2 (2006): article 25. http://www.webology.ir/2006/v3n2/a25.html.

McMillan, Sally J. and Margaret Morrison. "Coming of age with the Internet: A qualitative exploration of how the Internet has become an integral part of young people's lives." *New Media & Society* 8, no. 1 (2006): 73–95.

Merriam Webster. "Blog." *Merriam Webster Online Dictionary*, 2006. http://www.merriamwebster.com/dictionary/blog (accessed November 3, 2006).

Notess, Greg. "The terrible twos: Web 2.0, Library 2.0 and more." *Online* 30, no. 3 (2006): 40–42.

Open Source Initiative. History of OSI. Open Source Initiative: OSI http://www.opensource.org/docs/history.php (accessed November 3, 2006).

O'Reilly, Tim. "What is Web 2.0: Design patterns and business models for the next generation of software." *O'Reilly Website*, 2005a. http://www.oreillynet.com/pub/a/oreilly/tim/news/2005/09/30/what-is-web-20.html (accessed October 30, 2006).

———. "Web 2.0: Compact definition?" *O'Reilly Radar*, 2005b. http://radar.oreilly.com/archives/2005/10/web_20_compact_definition.html (accessed October 11, 2006).

Peek, Robin. "Web Publishing 2.0." *Information Today* 22, no. 10 (2005): 17–18.

Plutchak, T. Scott. "Why I dislike the Library 2.0 tag." [weblog entry] *T. Scott Blog*, January 5, 2006a. http://tscott.typepad.com/tsp/2006/01/why_i_dislike_t.html.

Plutchak, T. Scott. "Librarians Unnumbered." [weblog entry] *T Scott Blog*, April 12, 2006b. http://tscott.typepad.com/tsp/2006/04/librarians_unnu.html.

Rainie, Lee. "Digital Natives: How today's youth are different from their 'digital immigrant' elders and what that means for libraries." Presentation for Metro-New York Library Council, October 27, 2006. http://www.pewinternet.org/PPF/r/71/presentation_display.asp.

Rosenbush, Steve. "The MySpace ecosystem." *Business Week Online*, July 21, 2006. http://www.businessweek.com/technology/content/jul2006/tc20060721_833338.htm.

Soukup, Charles. "Computer-mediated communication as a virtual third place: building Oldenburg's great good places on the world wide web." *New Media & Society* 8, no. 3 (2006): 421–440.

SourceForge.net. "SourceForge.net: What is SourceForge.net?" *SourceForge.net* website, 2006. http://sourceforge.net/docs/about (accessed November 3, 2006).

Stephens, M. "Blogs (weblogs innovations)." *Library Technology Reports* 42, no. 4 (2006): 15–36.

UNESCO. Free Software History. *UNESCO Free Software Portal*. http://www.unesco.org/webworld/portal_freesoft/open_history.shtml (accessed November 7, 2006).

Wikipedia. "Wikipedia Statistics." *Wikipedia*. 2006. http://en.wikipedia.org/wiki/Special:Statistics (accessed November 6, 2006).

2

LOOKING TOWARD CATALOG 2.0

Michael Casey

Google is my homepage. It is the very first page I see every time I start my web browser. This is not to say that every time I start my web browser I perform a Google search. Quite often I don't. But Google has done a few things for me that make me keep it as a homepage. First, the Google search is excellent. I get good results and I am comfortable with the accuracy of its relevancy ranking. Second, the Google page is slim. Even if I do not perform a search I know that starting with Google as my homepage will not slow me down—it loads very quickly and is always up, therefore it is a very good indicator of whether or not my Internet connection is alive. I cannot say the same about the many aggregators, newspapers, or library pages I might otherwise choose as my homepage.

I mention Google at the beginning of this chapter because it sets the tone for where I see the library catalog going. You see, I am not a cataloger nor am I a programmer. I view myself simply as an end user, and as such I do not really care what has to go on behind the scenes in order to create the perfect catalog. The modern integrated library system (ILS) is far more than a catalog interface. But that fact seems to have clouded the reality that, though a small part of the ILS, the catalog is the face that customers see. Customers do not see the inventory management or acquisition side of the ILS; they only see the search or discovery side.

Designers of library catalogs often make the mistake of asking librarians what features are most important to library users, when in fact librarians have fundamentally different needs than the vast majority of end users. This can be seen in the very slow understanding among librarians and ILS vendors that what customers really wanted was relevancy ranking of results. Through the 1990s and into the twenty-first century, library catalog and search designers looked the other way when it came to Internet search engines. But far more people were searching the Internet than were using library catalogs. As the size of the web grew and grew, the amount of information available began to challenge the information available from the library. This chapter is not about the quality of that information but the competition to provide that information must be mentioned.

ROLE OF THE LIBRARY CATALOG

The role that the catalog plays, especially in the public library, has been subject to great change over the past few years. What was once simply a means to finding a book has since become a portal for library users to find electronic media, downloadable content, online resources, subscription databases, library services, and even local events. The catalog of twenty years ago that simply combed through machine-readable cataloging (MARC) records and returned status and location information has long since ceased being a viable library tool.

Until the mid-1990s, library catalogs were one of the few catalog interfaces that most people used. Before the advent of web commerce there were very few retail establishments that would require you to use an electronic catalog interface in order to search inventory. You simply walked into a store and bought items off the shelf. Libraries, by their very nature, required a more complicated management system, whether the card catalog of yesteryear or the online public access catalog (OPAC) that developed in the 1980s.

But the emergence of the World Wide Web in the 1990s brought forth a new generation of customer and it taught people that search and discovery did not have to be quite the painful process exemplified by library OPACs. Web users quickly began using the many new e-commerce sites that sprang up competing for their dollars. Sites such as CDNow.com and Amazon.com offered shoppers huge selections at bargain prices, and they made finding the items a simple task. Amazon.com went so far as to actually involve customers by allowing them to write reviews and add star ratings to products.

Throughout the early years of the web, users transitioned from directory structures, such as the early Yahoo!, to smarter and more powerful web searches as offered by Lycos, Alta Vista, Inktomi, and eventually, Google. The directory structure that Yahoo! founders David Filo and Jerry Yang began using to categorize the web quickly became too complicated and unwieldy, and search engines with better and better relevancy ranking soon began competing for top Internet billing. Google's quick rise to the top of the search engine field was due as much to its clean interface as to its superior PageRank algorithm. Search engine users appreciated the clean, simple, and fast-loading interface over the many other cluttered search engines and directories.

SLOW TO CHANGE

Library catalogs remained static and much unchanged during this period as ILS vendors were very slow to respond to the changing Internet marketplace. Librarians tried to adapt in the late 1990s by adding web page links within the catalog, often purchasing those services from third-party companies. But simply adding URLs to the catalog reflected the growing confusion within the profession regarding how to respond to the rapidly increasing importance of the Internet.

Librarians recognized the need to consolidate the many sources of information. But the catalog module that came with most ILS was inadequate to the task. The ILS database was but one information silo in a world full of proprietary and closed databases.

Working to resolve the multiple silos of information will take time. Any new catalog that tries to deal with these many information sources will have to have a very robust computer infrastructure. Having to scour many databases and many indexes takes computing power and, therefore, money. Interacting with these different sources also increases the chance for error and can result in a fragile end product. Current efforts to incorporate third-party products such as Radio Frequency Identification (RFID) and self-check into ILS systems illustrate the complexity of the problem. Getting third-party software to read and get along with other information sources does not always work as planned.

NEED FOR CHANGE

The more people used the Internet for search and e-commerce, the more these same people came to regard the library catalog as antiquated and obstructionist. Users became used to the Google spell checker, but library catalogs from most major ILS vendors did not offer spell checking for search queries. Search engines like Ask Jeeves prompted people to enter natural language searches, but library catalogs did not offer natural language search. And almost every search engine touted its superior relevancy ranking, but almost no library catalog offered quality relevancy sorting.

These strictly structured catalogs were also unidirectional—users had no way of supplementing keywords, adding reviews, etc. Customers began to notice the differences. A book search in Amazon.com would not only produce the requested item but would also provide customer reviews, starred aggregate ratings, alternate selections, and links to books that other people performing similar searches were buying. Amazon.com searches also included book cover art and would eventually allow customers to actually browse parts of the book itself. Suddenly Amazon.com was the library user's best friend. The sense of community and trust that Amazon.com was building was nowhere to be found in the local public library's OPAC.

But e-commerce sites were not the only ones that library users began comparing to library sites. Better design and tighter integration of museum collections such as the Metropolitan Museum of Art in New York and online movie encyclopedias like the Internet Movie Database had customers asking why library collections could not be as easily integrated into such a user-friendly interface. Going to the Met's website, browsing the upcoming events, examining images from the collection, and buying things from the online museum shop was seamless and tightly integrated. On the contrary, a visit to the average library website required seeing two or three different interfaces—the catalog, the library homepage, and perhaps an e-commerce add-on. Moving between the catalog and library events and services was not possible and this lack of ability was painfully obvious to every user.

Library catalogs were certainly not the only services being reexamined during this time. The changes wrought by the Internet were being felt by every business and service provider. New theories of business operations were being developed that pushed the end user to new heights of importance. Business 2.0, an idea and a magazine started in the late 1990s, argued that the new rules were fundamentally different and that businesses were operating in a completely unexplored environment than only a few years prior.

Retailers and service organizations were paying more attention to the attributes of Business 2.0—that physical presence is less important than how you are perceived, that distance between company and customer no longer matters, that people are the driving force, and that the market is getting more competitive because of the shrinking factors of time and space.

Libraries tied to ILS vendors began trying to modify their catalogs to better reflect customer expectations. This was not easy, however. Vendors were very slow to respond to librarian demands. Using old business models, many vendors try to sell add-ons such as spell checkers and e-mail notification systems. These "modules" were added cost and added complexity.

The advent of Web 2.0—referring primarily to the second generation of Internet-based services that almost always include some type of user participation—signaled a shift in Internet usability. No longer was the web simply a mass of static web pages pushing content out to users. The web was developing into a community, a two-way street filled with customer-created content, interconnectivity, browser-based applications, and a model of rapid change.

Rapid change is one of the things that customers almost never saw in library catalogs. ILS systems would plug along for five or ten or more years without major changes or upgrades. Interfaces shifted from being text-driven to graphical but little else of substance happened over the course of the 1990s and early 2000s.

The next version of the library catalog, or OPAC, whether it is a proprietary system crafted by a veteran ILS vendor or an open source system that allows tinkering and modifications, will have to include many of the attributes that comprise the definition of Web 2.0. User participation, customization, maximum usability, and greatly enhanced discovery are but four of the requirements.

What follows is a list of attributes that the next version of the library catalog, Catalog 2.0, should offer its users. None of the items on the list is cutting edge or revolutionary. Indeed, many of these things have been found on Internet search engines and other places on the web for many years. That fact should explain exactly how far behind library catalogs have fallen in relation to their online search cousins.

INGREDIENTS FOR CATALOG 2.0

Relevancy Ranking

Relevancy ranking in a traditional catalog would simply mean how often your term shows up in specific fields and how rare it is in the database as a whole. Search for a word that exists in only three records but in one record it appears twice as often as the other two records and there you have your relevancy.

Clean Interface (with Complex Options)

Look at almost any library catalog interface and you will see several search option choices—title, author, title keyword, etc. Many libraries default to one particular variation of keyword searching, but the typical user is not interested in choosing which type of strict word or keyword searching to perform—they simply want to enter their information and let the catalog's relevancy ranking determine the best match.

Results pages are often the same. Look at most results pages, even good ones like North Carolina State University's new online catalog using Endeca's ProFind platform, and you'll see a complex and slightly intimidating array of choices that are presented with your results. Now go to Amazon.com and perform the same search. You'll be presented with many of the same options—category narrowing, related search words, options to sort by different criteria, plus many options not seen on library catalogs such as rankings, reviews, excerpts, and more. But what Amazon.com is able to do with all of this is to present it in a cleaner fashion with cover art and a lot more immediate information.

Spell Checking

Spell checking is an absolute requirement for any search field anywhere. The fact that library ILS vendors have not yet made this standard in every product they sell is an embarrassment. That some think they can charge for it as an add-on is reason enough to find a new vendor.

Faceting

E-commerce sites like Zappos have been using faceting for years. Search for a pair of brown shoes and you can arrange your results by style, size, width, etc. Search for a book in Amazon.com and you can narrow your search by category keyword. Even cooking sites like Epicurious have offered faceted searching in the form of recipe categories, health options, main ingredients, course, etc. Being able to search and then browse by category is a powerful tool, but one that most library catalogs are without.

True Basic Search Field

Basic searching is not offering three fields and allowing customers to choose between title keyword, author keyword, or general keyword. Basic searching is one field that searches all parts of the MARC record, takes into account customer-added tags, positive and negative rankings, trust levels of those tagging and ranking, and recommendations, and then presents the results in relevancy order.

Advanced Searching

There will always remain the need for more advanced search operations. The Google advanced search screen and the Technorati advanced search page both offer very good examples of guided advanced searching. The Google page makes it very easy to limit by site type, date, etc., in a simple and easily understood way. The need for complex search interfaces that allow inline operators and Boolean searching is satisfied best by simply allowing those operations in the general search field, as Google currently does. If you know the syntax you can conduct a rather complex search from within the basic search field. What libraries need to ask is whether our users need this type of complex searching. Different library types will have different answers, but in the end what it really comes down to is how easy it is to use this search page. Design is almost as important as results because if it's not easy to use then no matter how powerful the search it will go unused. Guided advanced searching, when designed correctly, presents the user with the best of both worlds.

Full-text Searching of All Holdings (Not Simply Citations)

The more data you can search the better your odds of finding what you need. Being able to search the full text of books, rather than simply search their citations, more accurately reflects user understanding of how search engines operate. Google does not simply search website citations; it searches the entire website, finding a wealth of information that would otherwise be lost. Google's Book Search (http://books.google.com) is an excellent example of how this would work.

Reviews (Professional)

Some search catalogs are already providing links to professional reviews. Trusted sources such as School Library Journal reviews and Publisher's Weekly, along with other sources, provide the customer with a valuable decision making tool when exploring books.

Similar Searches (Others who Searched for This Also Searched for . . .)

Our customers are interested in what other people with similar interests and similar reading styles like to read. By providing this information we are building community.

User-added Tags

Tagging harnesses the knowledge of the users. It is at the heart of Web 2.0. User tagging is reflective of the way that people categorize information. Customers are comfortable using such sites as Flickr and del.icio.us to tag their own photos and links. Allowing them to tag catalog entries will aid discovery, increase usability, and is a low-cost alternative to customized local cataloging.

Customer-written Reviews

Customers love to talk about their favorite books, websites, etc. Allowing them to write reviews builds community, allows sharing, and creates a network of users. These reviews then help other library users find material by weighing the input of their community.

Blogs

Yes, even library catalogs need blogs. Build them into the system. Have genre blogs, author blogs, any type of blog that may interest enough people to communicate.

Option to Allow Reputation Ranking

Reputation ranking allows fellow catalog users to rate reviewers and taggers. Tags and reviews written by those with high reputations could possibly weigh more when considered against other rankings and reviews. Many sites utilize reputation scores, but perhaps the most popular use is by eBay.

Reputation tracking requires a willingness on the end user's part to give up some anonymity. Because of this, reputation ranking should be optional as an opt-in choice.

Aggregated Rating System

Like Amazon.com's star system, an aggregated rating system of user-created rankings for catalog entries would be yet another tool for users to apply when sorting search results.

Suggest to Friends Link (E-mail)

This is a simple mechanism to employ but a very good way for library catalog users to share information. This is especially helpful when you include more than simple materials in your catalog. Links to upcoming events, services, etc., can easily be shared by library customers.

RSS Feeds for the Catalog and Library Website

Again, this simple-to-employ but very powerful tool, allows customers to customize their information and stay informed about materials and services they are interested in. With RSS aggregators now built into the newest versions of almost every web browser the ability of library customers to tailor information in ways they need it is greater than ever. Customers interested in particular subject areas would be able to receive immediate updates when new materials appear that match their interest areas. Likewise, customers interested in specific library events and programming could receive such updates via RSS feeds. By crafting the library's web page so that it allows customized feeds the library customer could subscribe to specific feeds and have that information reflected directly on their customized library page. RSS feeds would serve both the end user—through aggregators or customized web pages—and the library—by making it easier to create and distribute library announcements to people interested in particular services.

Citation Creator for Various Formats

With the availability of online word processing the chances are rather high that a library customer will be using one of our library computers to write a paper. Why not make life easier for our users and provide automatic citations for every catalog entry?

CURRENT EFFORTS AT OPAC IMPROVEMENTS

North Carolina State University (NCSU) libraries recently began using Endeca's ProFind Guided Navigation software to interact with their ILS system. Endeca uses something called faceted metadata search to provide users with navigation links to alternative results based upon attributes of the search results. This type of search engine can point the user to alternative areas that they may not have considered or that they would have had to use an advanced search feature to find. Several other search engines use this method of search. The Library Corporation's AquaBrowser uses similar technology to provide a geographic representation of the user's search and possible alternatives.

Faceted metadata search is widely used in business, especially e-commerce, where helping customers successfully search product catalogs has an immediate financial return. If you search for a coat and instead find a jacket that you purchase then both you and the merchant are happy. Connecting the user with what they want—even if they are not clear on what they want—is perhaps the biggest feature in NCSU's Endeca search engine.

But the future of this type of application is unclear. That it sits on top of an existing, proprietary ILS means there will always be that limiting factor of complexity and expandability. Proprietary coding aside, the simple need to purchase and maintain two separate tools to provide one seamless search experience runs contrary to long-term efficiency. Long-term efficiency would have the data (the index) stored remotely and globally accessible to all libraries, everywhere. This would eliminate local customization but really, who has the time or money to do that anymore?

Hennepin County Public Library has taken several steps toward improving their catalog. They added the ability for customers to write reviews for items in the catalog and they also include recent reviews from Amazon.com. In addition, many of their titles include the first chapter, professional book reviews, and cover art.

Casey Bisson crafted something he calls WPopac—Wordpress OPAC—by overlaying Wordpress bogging software over top of his ILS. While simple on its surface, this small application allows commenting, RSS feeds, tagging, and just about everything else that any Wordpress installation can offer.

What is amazing about Bisson's creation is that it is relatively simple, open source, and easy to modify. The WPopac is able to make all of the underlying data available to any plug-in, thereby creating an almost limitless range of possible applications.

Google Book Search is helping libraries by including a "find this book in a library" link with every individual search result. The service uses several large union catalogs, including WordCat. Google Book Search also makes it possible to search library catalogs through advanced search, but the caveat there is that you are only searching the library catalog's metadata and not the scanned full-text of the book.

John Blyberg of the Ann Arbor District Library recently won an award for a gadget he wrote called Go-Go-Google Gadget. This "simple" group of four gadgets allows Ann Arbor customers to see what they have on hold, what they have checked out, all of the new books, and the top circulating books. The neat thing about these gadgets is that they allow the end users to decide how they want to use this information and they make it available outside of normal channels, meaning outside of the OPAC.

CONCLUSION

This list has but a few of the many suggestions currently being discussed for the next library OPAC. There are many others out there going farther than this in the breadth and depth of their OPAC recommendations. Karen Schneider, Casey Bisson, John Blyberg, Paul Miller, and many others all have very clear visions of what they want the next library catalog to include. What everyone probably agrees on however is that our current generation catalog is outdated. Whatever comes next has to include many more ways for our users to involve themselves in the overall OPAC experience, both in planning and in customizing; it has to be far more usable; and, it has to make discovery a far more rewarding experience.

WEBSITES

Google Book Search: http://books.google.com
Hennepin County Public Library: http://www.hclib.org/
North Carolina State University Library: http://www.lib.ncsu.edu/
Casey Bisson: WPopac: http://maisonbisson.com/blog/post/11133/
Ann Arbor District Library: http://www.aadl.org
Karen Schneider: http://freerangelibrarian.com/
John Blyberg: http://www.blyberg.net
Paul Miller: http://paulmiller.typepad.com/

3

THE WONDERFUL WORLD OF WIKIS: APPLICATIONS FOR LIBRARIES

Chad F. Boeninger

Many Library 2.0 concepts and technologies can enable libraries and librarians to communicate more effectively within a library organization and with the community that the library serves. A wiki is one such technology that libraries can use in different ways to meet the needs of the organization and the needs of patrons. A wiki is a flexible tool that libraries may use to promote internal communication, provide a virtual space for group collaboration, or create dynamic content for the user population. This chapter will discuss these three applications for wikis in libraries and will provide examples of each application. In demonstrating these applications, the chapter will also offer some lessons learned from personal experiences with using wikis and provide some suggestions for making the most out of wikis in libraries.

AN INTRODUCTION TO WIKIS

In its simplest terms, a wiki is basically a website in which the content can be created and edited by a community of users. Generally, a wiki is edited via a web interface, which allows users to update content without the need for specialized web authoring software or advanced HTML coding skills. Because a wiki can be edited by a community of users, the strength of the wiki often depends on the involvement of the community. Whereas traditional websites are created and maintained by an individual, wikis encourage community participation in creating and maintaining the website.

Like many web-based tools, wikis were first used by computer programmers to work collaboratively on projects. Each programmer could add and edit content to the wiki, regardless of his or her location. By adding content to the wiki, the programmers were creating a knowledge base that each individual could consult while working on his or her part of the programming project. These types of wikis have been around for quite some time, and they continue to be popular among developers in the open source software community.

Wikis became more mainstream with the creation and growing popularity of the Wikipedia (www.wikipedia.org). The Wikipedia, created in 2001, is a free encyclopedia that is written and edited collaboratively by people from all over the world. According to the Wikipedia itself, it is the largest reference website on the Internet today. Its popularity has caused some debate in the academic community as many librarians, educators, and researchers question the reliability of the encyclopedia's content. While the validity of information in the Wikipedia may be under constant scrutiny, the Wikipedia does serve as an excellent example of how wikis may be used to facilitate communication of information and promote community among users.

Groups, organizations, and companies have noticed the example that the Wikipedia provides and many have begun to create wikis of their own. One needs to only visit the Wiki Index (http://www.wikiindex.com) to discover that people have created wikis on almost any topic. As of this writing, the Wiki Index contains 3,200 wikis in a variety of areas. For example, a guitar player might visit the Guitar Wiki (http://guitarwiki.com); someone interested in sharing recipes might visit the Cookbook Wiki (http://www.cookbookwiki.com); and fanatics of the Muppets might visit the Muppet Wiki (http://muppet.wikia.com). Groups such as these have been able to take advantage of the wiki technologies and there are a variety of ways in which libraries can use wikis as well.

A WIKI FOR INTERNAL COMMUNICATION

One way that a library can use a wiki is for internal communication in the organization. Many libraries have staff intranets and web pages that are intended to be resources for library staff members. Many staff intranets are maintained by a single web administrator or a handful of other people who have access to the web server. While these intranets and web pages are usually developed with the best intentions, they can often become out-of-date because only a few people are adding and maintaining the content. A wiki can help alleviate this problem since anyone can add and edit content, thereby ensuring timely, relevant communication among the users.

An example of this type of wiki is the Ref Wiki that is used by the reference department at Ohio University's Alden Library. The reference department started using a wiki for departmental communication in June 2006. The Ref Wiki has replaced the blog that the department had used for internal communication purposes for over two years. As the content of the blog grew, its structure and organization began to decline. While the blog served the department well as a timely communication device, its magnitude made it difficult to use the resource as a knowledge base. The Ref Wiki was created as a means to organize and distribute departmental communication more effectively. Before the wiki, some content was in the departmental blog, while other documents, policies, and training materials were scattered in different folders on several network drives. In order to find out where a document was on the network drive, one had to search through multiple folders or ask the person who created and saved the document. Because locating a document often required human intervention, this was not the most effective way for the department to communicate.

The Ref Wiki contains a variety of information and the content continues to evolve as needed. The Ref Wiki currently contains information for those tough stumper questions and research assignments that the reference staff members are presented with each quarter. Since that information is in the wiki, rather than in an e-mail or networked drive, it is readily accessible at the time of need. The Ref Wiki also contains hints for dealing with various technology issues, such as how to resolve printing problems or basic use of an FTP client. The wiki serves as a place to put answers for staff-related FAQs, and it is also beginning to serve as a repository for department meeting minutes.

There are several advantages that a wiki has over e-mail lists, blogs, or network drives. One that has already been stated is that, because the wiki is on the Internet, it can be accessed from anywhere. To find the content, one simply has to access the wiki's web address, rather than be connected to network drive or e-mail folders. This allows users to access information from their office computers, from the reference desk, from the classroom, and even from home. Another highlight of using a wiki is that when content is added, that content immediately becomes part of a searchable knowledge base. Because most wikis rely on a database as the backend structure, the entire database can be searched with keywords. In most cases, the search results are displayed in order of descending relevancy. By contrast, the search results of a blog's content are usually displayed in reverse chronological order, which can make finding information among the results a little more difficult.

Some wiki software allows for the use of categories. The Ref Wiki takes advantage of this feature by allowing users to add categories as they create and edit wiki articles. The Ref Wiki has broad categories for technology, polices, troubleshooting, meeting minutes, and more. This allows a user simply to click on the category to browse all articles in that particular category. In this way, a user does not necessarily need to phrase what he or she is looking for in keyword terms, but can simply look in the category that is most relevant to the inquiry.

A final strength of the wiki for internal communication is it allows anyone to edit and create content. This works wonderfully for the Ref Wiki, because content can become out of date as quickly as a patron or colleague raises a new question. If such a situation occurs, then the staff member who answers the question can also update the content as needed in the wiki. Other staff members can review and edit the same content, so the knowledge and information shared in a wiki is truly a collaborative effort. If staff members are diligent about adding to the wiki, then it can offer relevant and timely information for its users.

A WIKI FOR INSTITUTIONAL COLLABORATION

Wikis can also be used to foster collaboration among the larger institution or community that the library serves. An example of this is the Ohio University Second Life Learning Community wiki (http://www.library.ohiou.edu/sllc). Second Life is a virtual world in which all content (avatars, buildings, businesses) are built by the participants. The Second Life Learning Community (SLLC) is a group of Ohio University faculty and staff from all over campus who are exploring and experimenting with how Second Life can be used to enhance the Ohio University academic and research environments. The group has been in operation since July 2006 and has only met in person on two occasions. The other meetings of the group are conducted in Second Life. At the first in-person meeting in July, one of the members inquired about how the group would communicate. She suggested that perhaps the group could use a wiki in order to keep the barrage of email to a minimum. As a member of the community, and as one who had experience with creating and maintaining wikis, I volunteered to create and host a wiki for the group on the library's web server.

Many libraries are constantly striving to position themselves at the center of the campuses and communities that they serve, and Ohio University Libraries is no exception. Hosting and maintaining a wiki is one small way that the library can be at the center of the learning community, even if the SLLC's meetings never occur anywhere near the brick and mortar building. A library-hosted wiki can enable the library to be at the center of the virtual meeting space while also serving as a knowledge base and repository for the learning community. Since many departments or organizations do not have their own web server space, a library with server space can allocate a small partition for the community.

Since the SLLC is still fairly new, there has not been a great deal of activity on the wiki. There are currently nine registered users with the majority of contributions coming from three of them. However, the learning community is gaining momentum with new members and partnerships. As a result, the SLLC wiki should continue to grow along with the community and continue to offer a collaborative environment for the exchange of ideas and knowledge.

A WIKI AS A RESEARCH GUIDE

While the ability to foster collaboration is one of the primary strengths of a wiki, another advantage is that wikis enable users to generate dynamic content. With the constantly shifting sources of information and the rising expectations of information consumers, it can be a challenge for librarians to meet the needs of researchers. However, a wiki can be used to create and manage dynamic content in order to meet their needs.

In order to promote library resources and services, many librarians create and maintain research guides. Research guides, also know as subject guides or pathfinders, most recently have been static HTML web pages that point researchers to the most appropriate resources in a subject area or research field. While librarians often have the best intentions when creating them, many subject guides become neglected and outdated very quickly. Multiple factors can contribute to the difficulty in keeping these research guides up-to-date. First, librarians often do not have specialized web-authoring software or HTML coding skills that they need to edit their own pages. This means that edits must be done by a library web manager. Because the web manager acts as intermediary to the web content, updates may not be done as quickly as needed. In many cases, a librarian may need to save multiple edits so that the web manager can make all the changes at once, rather than repeatedly requesting edits from the web manager. As a result, content can continue to grow further out of date while saving edits for a convenient time for the web manager. Using a wiki as a research guide can solve many of these barriers, as a wiki can enable and empower librarians to create and edit their own content whenever—and wherever—the need arises.

As the bibliographer for business and economics, I previously maintained three separate research guides in the area of business. Because of the quantity and variety of proprietary business resources, the guides were divided into areas for general business, marketing, and international business. To have one business guide would have proved overwhelming to the user, as the guide most likely would have given users severe cases of information overload. Unfortunately, there were several problems with having three separate research guides. One was that users often had to look in three different places for information. At the same time, there was some overlap with each guide, so if a single resource changed in some way, all three guides might require editing. Finally, the only way to search a guide was to use the "Find" or "Find on this page" feature of the browser, but this archaic search method could only be performed on one guide at time. Each of these problems caused frustration, and it got to the point that the guides were only updated once a year.

In the summer of 2005, as I prepared for the annual updates of the three research guides, I got an idea to experiment with putting the content of the research guides into a wiki. I had been experimenting with wiki software for a few months, but had never actually set up a live wiki before. I was very familiar with the Wikipedia, but I had difficulty in seeing how something like that could be scaled down for a library application. However, my views changed after I saw the ALA Conference Wiki and The LibSuccess Wiki (www.libsuccess.org) that Meredith Farkas had created in the spring of 2005. After seeing these excellent models for wikis, I began to understand how a wiki might be used to replace my three research guides.

In June 2005, I installed the MediaWiki software on our web server. I chose MediaWiki simply because it was the same software that the Wikipedia uses, and I reasoned that future development of this open source application would be vibrant in order to support the free encyclopedia. After installing the software, I began populating the wiki with some of the best content from my three research guides. While transferring the content, which was a simple cut-and-paste exercise, I was able to weed out resources and information that I had not used in quite some time. At the same time, I was able to add value to listings for each resource by adding additional information. For example, rather than simply give a call number, title, and description of a reference book, I would actually try to write something about how each resource might be used. This process was quite slow, as it took me some time to write longer descriptions of each resource. While adding the content to the wiki, I was also creating the structure of the wiki at the same time. Since this was my first experience creating a wiki, I learned about the structure and organization as I added content. In adding the content, I assigned many of the resources in the wiki to categories, which helps to make the wiki more organized and usable.

In July 2005, the Biz Wiki (http://www.library.ohiou.edu/subjects/bizwiki) made its debut. As the description states, the Biz Wiki is a collection of resources available to business researchers at Ohio University and it is designed to assist them with their research. The Biz Wiki contains a variety of content, including information about reference books, websites, research guides, how-to documents, and more. The first type of content in the wiki, reference content, basically lists important reference books and websites for business research. An example of a reference article in the Biz Wiki is the article for the *Regional Encyclopedia of Business & Management*. This article lists the location and type of resource (reference book) and gives extensive information about what is covered in the resource. The information in the article is derived from the table of contents and introduction of the book, and is a great deal more comprehensive than the catalog record for the resource. The catalog record gives the subject headings (business—encyclopedias and management—encyclopedias), but that is a little too broad for this resource. By adding more information from the table of contents, as well as thoughts about how the item can be used, the article in the Biz Wiki can perhaps be a little more useful to the business researcher.

Another type of content in the Biz Wiki is more instructional in nature. Examples of this instructional content are the *Company Research Basics* and *Industry Research Basics* articles. These articles show the reader how to find particular types of information. They mention specific resources in the wiki and are cross-linked with those pages. Instead of lists of resources, the articles attempt to demonstrate why a particular resource might be valuable to users when researching a particular topic. Other articles, such as those for *Swot Analysis* and *Market Share*, define a particular business topic and show where to find information about that topic.

One of the major strengths of a wiki is the ability to add and edit content from anywhere. While this has already been discussed in terms of using wikis for internal communication, this feature is even more important when using a wiki as a research guide. Since a wiki is edited via a web interface, a librarian can create and maintain dynamic content from the office, the reference desk, the instruction lab, and even from home. The Biz Wiki is often edited from the reference desk, as questions from patrons often lead me to learn about different resources or force me to use resources in a different way. The resources that were used to answer the questions often make excellent content for the Biz Wiki. And since the wiki can be edited from anywhere, content can be added immediately.

Once content is added to the Biz Wiki, it is immediately searchable and usable by the end user. Most wikis have a keyword search box, and the Biz Wiki is no exception. A user simply has to enter a keyword, and matching results will be displayed in order of relevancy. The results even include key words in context that show where the search terms occurred in an article. The Biz Wiki uses MediaWiki software, so the search interface and results list are very similar to that of the popular Wikipedia. Users who find a relevant article in the wiki can be pointed to other information from within the article. The MediaWiki software makes it easy to assign categories to an article, and clicking on a category will take the user to other similar information. For example, users searching the Biz Wiki for "buying power" will find the article for *Demographics USA*, since "buying power" is in the description for the resource. The user will then notice that the article for *Demographics USA* is in the Demographics and Market Data categories, and clicking on the "Demographic" category will take the user to nine other related resources. In a sense, this functions the same way as the keyword to subject heading search strategies that librarians teach when demonstrating article databases and catalogs.

Most librarians would love to see how their research guides are being used. With traditional HTML pages, hits can be measured by looking at the web server logs or by using a hit tracker. The MediaWiki software has a built-in function that measures each time a page is accessed. This feature, called Popular Pages, allows the viewing of all the pages in the wiki ranked in terms of popularity. With the Biz Wiki, it is easy to determine which pages are used the most. This can influence what type of

THE WONDERFUL WORLD OF WIKIS

content the librarian will add in the future, and may even have implications for what type of materials the librarian purchases. Since the Biz Wiki went live in July 2005, the front page has been accessed over 39,000 times. The most popular articles include the Industry Research Basics and Company Research Basics guides, each receiving more than 8,300 and 7,900 hits since being created in January 2006. Finally, of the 111 articles in the Biz Wiki, 69 have been accessed more than 1,000 times.

BEST PRACTICES FOR LIBRARY WIKIS

The Biz Wiki is a resource that has proved to be very popular with business re-searchers at Ohio University. The success of the Biz Wiki has led to the creation of the Ref Wiki and the SLLC, which were previously discussed, and it has given other librarians ideas about how wikis might be used at their institutions. If libraries or librarians would like to create a wiki of their own, there are several factors to consider. The first thing is to question whether or not a wiki is really needed at all. Granted, wikis are very cool tools, but a library does not need a wiki just because everyone else is getting one. To begin, a library might want to determine in what way a wiki is needed. Will the wiki help communication in the organization? Will the wiki help to fill some void or solve some problem? Is there a need for virtual collaborative spaces? Does the library need to disseminate dynamic content to library users? Only if a wiki is needed should the library spend the time and energy in starting one.

If there is indeed a need for wiki, librarians should look at other wikis to see how they might incorporate some ideas, organizations, structure, and even content into their own wikis. They might even try contacting the wiki creators to learn what has worked and what has not. Many people are very willing to share what they have learned along the way. One place to look for examples of other wikis is the Wiki Index (http://www.wikiindex.com), a directory of "wikis, wiki people, and wiki ideas." With more than 3,000 wikis in the index, it is good place to find some great examples.

Once a vision or mission for a wiki has been established, the next step is to investigate software options for the wiki. While this chapter has documented experiences with MediaWiki, there are a number of other options available. There are essentially two different types of wiki software. The first option is a self-hosted application such as MediaWiki. With a self-hosted wiki, the library would need to select a software application and install it on the library's web server. While many of the software options are open source and free, the real cost to the library is in the manpower and technical expertise that is needed to install and maintain a self-hosted wiki. Self-hosted wikis require knowledge of MySQL and PHP, and some experience with web server administration. The wiki administrator must also keep the wiki software up-to-date, as new versions with enhancements, bug fixes, and security patches are released regularly. While it may seem like a lot of work, there are numerous advantages to hosting a wiki on the library's own server. With a self-hosted wiki, the data and all wiki files are stored locally. The library is not dependent on a wiki-hosting service to maintain the data or even the service. Also, hosting a wiki on the library's server generally allows the wiki administrators access to all wiki files, which makes it easier to customize the wiki's look and design, while also adding optional plug-ins and extensions.

While a locally-hosted wiki certainly has a number of advantages, many libraries do not have the technical expertise or the time required to create and maintain a wiki on their own servers. If this is the case, then libraries may wish to pursue services that offer wiki hosting options. These services, often referred to as wiki farms, allow users to create and host a wiki on a company's server. Many of these services offer basic plans for free. One popular service, PBwiki (http://pbwiki.com), claims that making a wiki is as easy as making a peanut butter sandwich. To get started with PBwiki, one simply has to create a sitename and provide an e-mail address. PBwiki has a lot of documentation to help get a wiki started as well. While the service is very easy to use, one drawback is that it does not have the same customization options as a self-hosted wiki.

It may be difficult to choose between a fully configurable self-hosted option versus the easy-to-use and no-experience-required wiki service. To help choose the best software or service option for a wiki, librarians may wish to consult the WikiMatrix (http://www.wikimatrix.org/). The WikiMatrix allows users to select multiple wiki applications and compare them side by side. The site even has a "Choice Wizard" that will help users narrow down applications and software options based on selected criteria. It is advisable to try a number of options before committing to an application because it may be difficult to switch an established wiki to another software option or service.

After choosing a software or service option and installing or creating a wiki, the real work begins. One of the mistakes that many wiki creators make is turning a wiki over to its users too soon. It is strongly advised that the wiki creator should begin adding content and structure. Wikis are very new to many people, and if they are presented with a blank wiki with little structure, they may not be inclined to add to it. In many cases, people will be afraid to add new content to a blank wiki, simply because they may not know if their content is the right kind of content to add. To help get a wiki started right, the wiki's creator needs to add content and structure so that users will have examples to refer to when adding their own content.

At the same time, the wiki creator might want to create some type of documentation that tells users what the wiki is for, how it can be used, and how to add and edit content. Many wiki software applications contain a default help page that can be edited to meet the needs of the specific wiki. The Ref Wiki contains flash tutorials that demonstrate how to add and edit content. Wiki administrators might also create a "sandbox" space in the wiki and link to the sandbox from the wiki's front page. This sandbox can serve as a place for new wiki users to try adding and editing content without the worry of breaking anything.

The primary strength of a wiki is its ability to allow contributions from anyone in the community. Unfortunately, many wiki administrators are hesitant about opening a wiki up for community editing. It is often difficult for a wiki creator to give up control to the community, but it is necessary for the wiki to be a truly collaborative resource. A wiki creator needs to refrain from worrying too much about the structure and content of the wiki. Of course, he or she needs to make sure that no inappropriate content is placed on the wiki, but if the wiki community is active the users will take care of removing that kind of material. In addition, the wiki creators should not be surprised if they find that their wiki is being used differently than originally intended. Once again, the wiki will be used as the community best sees fit. As an example, the Biz Wiki was originally designed so that faculty, staff, and students at Ohio University could add and edit content. However, since its inception in July 2005, no one has added any content. This was initially disappointing, but the usage statistics show that the user community is happy just using the resource and not contributing to it.

A final suggestion is that librarians need to have realistic expectations for a wiki. People are generally slow to adopt new technologies, and wikis are no exception to this rule. Librarians should not be discouraged if a wiki is not used as much or if the community is not contributing as expected. Rather, librarians should take every opportunity to promote the wiki to the community of users. It may take some time, but eventually users will learn to appreciate the innovation and understand the usefulness of the wiki.

As collaborative tools, wikis offer a great deal of flexibility to both wiki creators and users. While this chapter has only discussed three applications of wikis in libraries, there are a number of other possibilities for using wikis. Wikis can empower librarians to communicate more effectively, help them to work collaboratively, and enable them to create dynamic content. All that a librarian needs is a vision, some creativity, and a desire to explore something new.

SUGGESTED READINGS

Boeninger, Chad F. "A Wiki as a Research Guide." *Library Voice*. July 13, 2005. http://libraryvoice.com/archives/2006/07/13/using-a-wiki-as-a-research-guide-a-years-experience/ (accessed November 14, 2006).

——. "Using a Wiki as a Research Guide: a Year's Experience." *Library Voice*. July 13, 2006. http://libraryvoice.com/archives/2005/07/13/a-wiki-as-a-research-guide/ (accessed November 14, 2006).

Farkas, Meredith. "So You Want to Build A Wiki?" *WebJunction*. September 1, 2005. http://webjunction.org/do/DisplayContent?id=11262 (accessed November 14, 2006).

——. "Using Wikis to Create Online Communities." *WebJunction*. September 1, 2005. http://webjunction.org/do/DisplayContent?id=11264 (accessed November 14, 2006.)

——. "Wiki White Paper" *TechEssence*. April 8, 2006. http://techessence.info/socialsoftware/wiki (accessed November 14, 2006).

Stephens, Michael. "Wikis." Chapter 5 in *Web 2.0 & Libraries: Best Practices for Social Software*. Chicago, IL: American Library Association, 2006.

4

PODCASTING IN LIBRARIES

Chris Kretz

Whether considered as a distribution technology, a format, or a phenomenon, pod-casting has come a long way in a short time. Even by the accelerated standards of the Internet, podcasting has quickly gone from the purview of a small number of programmers and bloggers to the beginning of what many consider to be a communications revolution. The ability to record and distribute audio content unfettered across the Internet affords everyone the chance to be the producer and host of their own "radio show." A wide range of people from hobbyists to newlyweds to former MTV hosts have quickly seized the opportunity to become a personal media outlet, creating entertaining and informative shows on topics that would never have been developed by traditional media (Farivar 2004). The astounding rate at which this has happened "makes even Moore's Law seem sluggish" (Campbell 2005, 44).

The word "podcasting" first appeared in print in February 2004 (Hammersley), minted from a combination of "broadcasting" and "iPod."[1] The term marries Apple's best-selling and near-ubiquitous iPod MP3 player to the practice of audioblogging, the posting of audio files on a blog. By April of 2005, a Pew Internet & Life Report (Rainie and Madden) found that over 6 million people had listened to a podcast.[2] Just over a year later, another study predicted nearly 60 million listeners by 2010 (Diffusion Group 2005).

Just as podcasting rose out of blogging, it first attracted attention in the library field through the biblioblogosphere. This loose yet interconnected network of tech-nologically aware librarian bloggers routinely discussed and debated developing issues and trends in the profession. These bloggers began debating the applicability of pod-casting to libraries. While many expressed interest in and even uploaded a handful of trial podcasts and audioblog posts, the question of whether or not the practice would become a trend in the larger library community remained in doubt.[3] Jane Balas, in her annual review of technology trends, offered cautious optimism while noting: "[t]his medium is so new that not even the podcasters themselves claim to know how it will evolve" (2005, 32).

THE TECHNOLOGY OF PODCASTS

The New Oxford American Dictionary definition of a podcast is "a digital recording of a radio broadcast or similar program, made available on the Internet for download- ing to a personal audio player."[4] This definition obscures the finer technical details that make podcasting an innovative development. While audio files and streaming media have been available on the Internet for years, what podcasting represents is a new delivery mechanism. It is a way to syndicate content and make it automatically available to remote subscribers. The actual location of the audio file, as well as the time and date of its posting, becomes a moot point as far as the listener is concerned. It is an automatic, anonymous, and (to date) free delivery system of audio on demand.[5]

There are three steps in this system of podcasting syndication:

1. An audio file is uploaded to the web.
2. An RSS 2.0 feed is associated with the file and also uploaded to the web.
3. The feed is read by a podcatcher application, which then downloads the audio file.

The Really Simple Syndication (RSS) feed is a simple text file written in XML (Extensible Markup Language) that sits on a server alongside the audio file. RSS is a popular method of delivering text-based information on the web. It was not until RSS version 2.0 with its use of enclosure tags that audio files could be delivered in the same way. The enclosure carries the URL of the audio file along with metadata on its size and file type.

The final step in the podcast chain, the podcatcher or podcast aggregator, is an application that reads RSS feeds and downloads the enclosed audio files. As new episodes of a podcast are put online, those URLs are added to the podcast's feed and any podcatcher that is subscribed to that feed will automatically recognize and download them.

Although use of the term podcast has been loosely applied to any audio file posted online, even where no RSS feed exists, the distinction is not to be overlooked. The RSS feed defines the podcast. For the end user, it is the metaphorical difference between having the *New York Times* waiting for them on the breakfast table every Sunday morning and having to wake up, get dressed, and trudge to the store to buy it.

What the definition of podcast does not include is any mention of the word iPod. No particular brand of device is necessary to listen to a podcast; it can be downloaded and played right off of a computer's desktop, transferred to a mobile MP3 player, or even burned to a CD.

EMERGING USES

Library podcasting on the institutional level did not begin until the appearance of "Listen Up!"—a podcast from the Decatur Campus Library of Georgia Perimeter

College in February 2005. Since then podcasts have appeared from a number of institutions, covering the spectrum of library types. The prevalent conception of a podcast as a radio show, while not always accurate, is a useful model for discussing how libraries have approached podcasting.

What follows is an overview of the types of podcasts that have been produced to date by both libraries and individual librarians. To avoid confusion, a library's *podcast* is taken to mean one RSS feed with all of its related content. A library may have multiple feeds and hence multiple podcasts. The audio files that get continually added to the feed are considered episodes. Examples here are drawn from the library's overall use of their podcast as well as experimental uses made from episode to episode. This list is not meant to be exhaustive but rather illustrative of existing uses, noting the unique and salient points of each.

The term podcast, although initially applied to an audio file, has evolved. Two variations have developed to date:

1. *Enhanced podcasts*: an audio podcast that includes images and URLs. These images and links are set to display at specific points during the audio on a computer screen or media player.

2. *Videocasts* or *vodcasts*: audio and video.

Booktalks

The booktalk format is tailor-made for podcasting, being short, concise, and self-contained. "BookTalks Quick and Simple," a podcast from New Hampshire School librarian Nancy Kean, features booktalks covering titles appropriate for grades K-12. Released on a nearly daily basis, each episode of the podcast is under 3 minutes.

The Hopkinton High School Library in Contoocook, New Hampshire, produces the "Isinglass Booktalk Podcasts." These are booktalks centered on titles nominated for the Isinglass Teen Read Award, which is bestowed annually by seventh and eighth graders in New Hampshire. Librarian Shelly Lockhead introduces each episode with background on the Awards and news from the library. The booktalks are conducted by library assistant Janet Plummer.

Displays and Exhibits

Podcasts can be used to enhance and expound upon exhibits currently on view as well as provide a surrogate experience for those who cannot physically visit the library.

"The Library Channel," a podcast from the Arizona State University Libraries, devotes an episode to an exhibit called Guarding the Flame, highlighting their collections of Sri Lankan monographs and palm leaf manuscripts. In an interview, South East Asian specialist bibliographer Christopher Miller explains the significance of the collections, their value to researchers, and the issues involved in their use and preservation.

While hosting the National Library of Medicine's traveling exhibit *Frankenstein: Penetrating the Secrets of Nature*, the Booth Library at East Illinois University (EIU) took on the ambitious task of recording a podcast version of Mary Shelley's original text. Broken into twenty-seven episodes, their unabridged reading of *Frankenstein* was released on a nearly daily schedule over a 1-month period. The podcast features the voices of EIU faculty and librarians as well as members of the local community.

Individual Librarians' Podcasts

True to the audioblogging roots of podcasting, the first library-related podcast appeared on the personal blog of a librarian. In January 2005, Gregg Schwartz, a public librarian and writer of the blog Open Stacks, began the "Open Stacks" podcast. On it he discusses library-related news gathered from journals and newspapers, comments on new research and developments in the field, and occasionally reports on conferences he has attended.

Jim Miles, associate dean for Legal Information Services and director of the Charles B. Sears Law Library at the University at Buffalo Law School, produces a weekly podcast called "Check This Out!" He talks frequently about issues in law librarianship and librarianship in general as well as personal interests such as film and music. "Check This Out!" is notable for its variety of content; episodes have included lunchtime roundtable interviews with colleagues, soundseeing and video tours of new library facilities, reports from Canadian and Technical Services correspondents, and a virtual call-in birthday celebration.

"Library Geeks" is an interview podcast produced by Dan Chudnov, Systems Programmer at the Yale Center for Medical Informatics. The podcast features Chudnov conducting telephone and in-person interviews with those involved in the study and development of technology in libraries. The episodes are lengthy, often over 60 minutes, but are valuable, information-rich glimpses into topics such as Functional Requirements for Bibliographic Records (FRBR), link resolvers, and online communities.

Interactive Podcasts

Although it has been noted that podcasts are not a vehicle for "two-way interaction or audience participation," (Educause 2005) there are ways to use them to create an interactive experience as well as to solicit feedback from listeners.

The Manchester Public Library's teen podcast "Prime Speaks" offered a unique tie-in with their Summer 2006 Teen Reading Program. Each year the program creates a t-shirt with a reading-related slogan written in a foreign or fictional language. An image of the 2006 slogan is included on one episode in the metadata field usually reserved for a song's album cover art. The image displays in the media player as the episode reveals that the language used is from a book previously mentioned on the podcast. For each correct guess as to the slogan's meaning, listeners are entered into a drawing for an iPod nano.

The Public Library of Charlotte & Mecklenburg County (PLCMC) in North Carolina dedicates two episodes of their teen podcast featuring scavenger hunts. Each includes instructions for finding clues in either the Myers Park Branch or the Imaginon building operated jointly by PLCMC and The Children's Theatre of Charlotte. Narrated by a group of teenagers, the episodes guide listeners from catalog entries to book titles to the Dewey Decimal system, finally arriving at an answer to be given to the librarian on duty in exchange for a prize.

In New York, Dowling College Library's "Omnibus" podcast contains two episodes incorporating use of a call-in line. The episodes, which feature interviews with teaching faculty discussing courses in film noir and Alfred Hitchcock, invite listeners to call in and leave a review of any of the films mentioned on the episode. The call-in line is part of the free unified messaging service provided by a company called K7. The service, which is used by many mainstream podcasts, converts voicemail messages into WAV files that are then delivered to an e-mail address. While the length of each message is limited to five minutes, the service provides an easy way to solicit listener feedback, comments, and even reports from off-site events.

Library Education

LISRadio at the School of Information Science and Learning Technologies at the University of Missouri-Columbia is a well-developed program of podcasts involving current faculty, students, and alumni. There are currently nine separate feeds, each with its own focus. "On The Job" interviews alums that have joined the library workforce, while the Graduate Student Association's podcast offers recordings of its regular meetings. "First Tuesday" is a monthly interview program with leading figures in the library field. LISRadio is a good example of how library schools can begin to provide students with the training and experience necessary to continue podcasting in the library profession.

Library Instruction

Podcasting has been applied to the educational mission of libraries to instruct users not only in the use of library resources but in general information literacy and use of new technologies as well.

The George C. Gordon Library at Worcester Polytechnic Institute (WPI) in Worcester, Massachusetts, produces a podcast called "Library Audio to Go." Focusing on specific information resources and topics related to library research, each episode is short, to the point, and presented in a conversational manner. The segment on patent searching, for example, uses WPI alum Robert Goddard and his career developing rockets as a framework for instruction. Other episodes include explanations of fire codes, 10 K filings, and the differences between WorldCat and the library's OPAC. Most of the shows are narrated by Christine Drew, the manager of Instruction and Outreach.

Andrea Bartelstein, Instructional Services Coordinator and Librarian for Education and Counseling, serves as narrator for the "Sheridan Libraries Podcasts" from Johns Hopkins University. Many of the episodes include interviews with librarians in various departments explaining how best to use the library's holdings. Shows have covered cartographic resources from the government publications, maps, and law library, an introduction to the Web of Science database, and a look at JHSearch, a federated search engine developed at Johns Hopkins.

The Providence Public Library's "Computer Tips" is an enhanced podcast featuring computer teacher Shane Sher. Episodes provide a hands-on tutorial for such popular resources as Google Earth, Flickr, and Craigslist. Listeners can follow along with changing screenshots that demonstrate what is being described on the audio.

Library News

In addition to the traditional newsletter and the library blog, podcasts have been used to keep users up-to-date on changing conditions at the library, current issues, and upcoming events.

"Listen Up!" is the podcast created by the Decatur Campus Library of Georgia Perimeter College. It serves as a current awareness tool for the campus community. Hosted by David Free, Public Services Librarian, "Listen Up!" provides news on upcoming library and campus events, reviews of new books, tips on using databases, and announcements of special hours of operation. Additional segments feature talks with staff and administrators from the library as well as related college services such as the Learning & Tutoring Center.

The Sunnyvale Public Library in California has also used its podcast to keep their community informed. One episode of the Sunnyvale Public Library podcast is dedicated to the communications officer of the city of Sunnyvale interviewing library director Deborah Barrow. Over the course of the interview, they discuss the role of the library in the community, the importance of usage statistics, matters of funding, and Sunnyvale's Library of the Future project.

Live Programs

Podcasting live events after the fact, as an audio or video recording, is an effective way of extending their reach and value. The time-shifted nature of podcasts allows those who cannot physically be present at an event to experience it at a later date, and the recordings also serve as a record of library activities. It is important to note that the nature of lectures and live programs often result in longer podcast episodes, typically lasting an hour or more.

The Claude Moore Health Sciences Library at the University of Virginia presents an annual History of the Health Sciences lecture series. Speakers touch on a number of topics relating to the history of medicine and health services, covering such varied and unique subjects as the demise of the iron lung and the health issues of black soldiers during the Civil War. The library has been recording these talks and releasing them as podcast episodes.

The Pritzker Military Library, a privately funded library in Chicago devoted to the study of military history and the "citizen soldier," offers a series of podcasts that present recordings of their live programs. The three podcasts to which listeners can subscribe individually or as one combined feed are: "The Medal of Honor Series," featuring interviews with Medal of Honor winners; "Tonight at the Pritzker Library," with talks by visiting authors of military fiction and nonfiction; and "Front and Center with John Callaway," a program in which journalist John Callaway interviews guests on pressing military topics.

The Westerville Public Library in Ohio produces a videocast of selected programs offered at the library. Episodes to date include visits from zoo animals and home remodeling workshops. The Kankakee Public Library in Illinois records the audio of its live programming for use in its podcast. Most episodes focus on visiting author talks, but other notable speakers have included Arlo Guthrie and a survivor of the Dresden firebombing.

Local History

Public libraries have long maintained local history collections and rooms devoted to their display and research. Likewise, archives and special collections at academic institutions help preserve the memory of the school and often the surrounding region. Podcasting offers a new and effective way of communicating that history as well as the library's role in its collection and preservation.

Worcester Polytechnic Institute in Worcester, Massachusetts, offers a unique, close-ended podcast drawn from the book *Two Towers: The Story of Worcester Tech 1865–1965.* Serialized over thirteen episodes, each chapter of the book is read by a librarian, faculty member, or administrator.

Dowling College's "Omnibus" devotes a number of episodes to interviews with local historians, researchers, and collectors of local history on the south shore of Long Island, New York. Additionally, recordings of dramatic readings of archival sources have been combined to form narrative histories of the college, using the voices of librarians and campus members.

The Sunnyvale Public Library in California has converted a number of existing oral histories into podcast episodes. Recordings from "Sunnyvale Voices: From Settlers to Silicon," an oral history project completed in 2000, were digitized and released as podcast episodes. These recordings showcase local residents reminiscing about the area's agricultural past and its changing landscape.

Organizational Podcasts

A number of professional library organizations have created podcasts to further their institutional mission, inform their members, and promote libraries in general.

PALINET, the organization of libraries and related institutions serving the Middle Atlantic States, produces two podcasts featuring interviews with prominent members of the library profession. "Technology Conversations" involves leading researchers and program developers in the library field discussing the latest topics. "IR Conversations" focuses on those involved in building and maintaining institutional repositories and the issues they face.

The New Jersey Library Association (NJLA) uses podcasting as a means of member education and promotion. During the 2006 annual NJLA conference, their Information Technology section created a podcast booth offering attendees a hands-on lesson in podcasting. Using a laptop and microphone, they recorded brief snippets from volunteers. The result is a podcast with over seventy episodes, each one being the recorded remarks of a conference participant.

Professional Development

OPAL (Online Programming for All Libraries) is a network of libraries dedicated to providing free online professional development opportunities to the library community. Although the programs are initially presented as live events, the audio of selected talks is subsequently released as an episode on their podcast. Presentations currently available include discussions of censorship, rural libraries, and collaboration among academic libraries.

The SirsiDynix Institute offers a series of online seminars, programs, and workshops for professional development within the library field. Similar to OPAL, their events take place in real time and are then released as podcasts. Past episodes cover such topics as gaming in libraries, screencasting, and conflict management.

Story Time

Another prevalent use of podcasting is as an extension of the traditional story time program. These podcasts can be either a recording of a live story time reading before an audience or a segment recorded by an individual librarian for release straight to a podcast.

The Denver Public Library offers podcasts of short nursery rhymes, fairy tales, and children's stories as recorded by librarians. The Orange County Library System offers a similar podcast with their "Children's Podstory." Episodes featuring storyteller Charlie Hoeck add local flavor with folk tales and legends such as the Hairy Man from Tombigbee River Swamp.

"Storytime" is a videocast from the Providence Public Library in Rhode Island. Each episode features a children's librarian reading a book to the camera. Guest readers from the Trinity Repertory Company of Providence have also been used.

The Teen Show

With the youth-driven image of the iPod, it is no surprise that a number of teen-centered podcasts have been developed out of public libraries' young adult departments.

The Cheshire Public Library in Connecticut produces the "Cheshire Public Library Podcast" that they describe as "a teen-driven cultural magazine." Each episode is an antic mix of movie, book, and music reviews, comedy skits, poems, man-in-the-street interviews, and other surprises. Teen librarian Sarah Kline Morgan is credited as producer and speaks on a number of segments, but most of the content is written and spoken by local teenagers. Promos for library and local events, as well as listener-submitted "shout outs" to friends are interspersed throughout. Participants are identified by name within each segment and contributors are listed in closing credits.

The "OCLS Teen Podcast" from the Orange County Library System in Florida has focused mostly on storytelling, with urban legends involving bugs, corpses, and pet rabbits recited by librarians to great effect. Other episodes include booktalks on young adult fiction and promos for upcoming events. One notable variation is an episode featuring a videocast advertising library game night. The 31-second video features footage of teens playing DDR (Dance Dance Revolution) inside the library. A driving drumbeat in the background adds to the sense of excitement and provides a strong pull for the program.

"Prime Speaks" is a book review podcast created out of the Teen Services department at the Manchester Public Library in Manchester, Connecticut. Each episode is a short review of titles appropriate for young adults delivered by the on-air persona of the teen services librarian, "Prime." Additional reviews are provided by teens using similar monikers. Manchester also provides a videocast version, under the title "Prime's Box Live."

Tours

"Soundseeing" tours were an early development of podcasting among the general public. These mobile recordings are made in a variety of places, from walks around a neighborhood to tours of specific sites such as museums (Kennedy 2005). To date this has been most frequently adapted by larger academic libraries, with podcast tours describing the physical layouts and collections of their buildings.

With 7 floors and 2.5 million items, the Alden Library at Ohio University is a perfect venue for a soundseeing tour. Their "Behind the Desk" podcast features an episode with a 16-minute tour including information on the library's collections, tips on using their services, and a brief introduction to the Library of Congress classification system. The tour is available in three versions: one narrated by a librarian, one by a student, and one in Swahili.

The Loyola Marymount University Library podcast features a 10-minute audio tour of the three floors of the Charles Von der Ahe Library. The tour is an enhanced podcast, with embedded images of library locations that change as the tour progresses. The audio provides physical descriptions of the building as well as an introduction to the services available on each floor.

ISSUES AND DECISIONS FOR LIBRARY PODCASTERS

The decision to podcast is not to be taken lightly and not without careful consideration of the issues involved. There are legal, technical, and conceptual questions to be anticipated and addressed before proceeding.

Legal Issues

Despite the name, podcasting is not broadcasting and does not require a Federal Communications Commission (FCC) license. It does, however, carry legal implications for the library in regard to such issues as copyright, libel, and slander. Legal advice should be consulted, but general procedures should include:

1. Getting signed permission from speakers to record and redistribute their presentations.
2. Permission from authors and artists to use any of their works on a podcast (both audio and video).
3. Permission for any music used. Luckily, podcasting has given rise to "podsafe music," music especially licensed to be used on podcasts. A number of online sites provide access to large collections of free podsafe music.

Presentation

Podcasting, of all the social software applications currently considered under the umbrella of Library 2.0, offers perhaps the best example of the tenet "the library is

Human" (Stephens 2005). It allows the library to present its staff and services in the voice of an actual person, to an audience that extends well beyond the reference desk. Questions to consider when planning how best to approach a podcast are:

1. Who will be speaking on the podcast? Speaking styles and ability vary, so a library must decide if they are looking for the most polished voice, the most interesting voice, a regional accent, or a number of different voices.

2. What tone will the podcast strike? There are many ways to set the tone of a podcast. Is the pace quick or slow? Does the library podcast speak with passion or objectivity? Humor or reserve?

3. How long should it be? There is no optimal length for a podcast, although longer episodes translate into large media files requiring more storage space and possibly longer download times.

Promotion and Branding

Getting the word out about a library podcast is essential. There are a number of steps that can be taken to ensure that listeners find the podcast and also recognize the library's role in producing it.

1. A podcast's RSS feed should be submitted to as many podcast directories as possible. Be forewarned that iTunes has developed its own customized tags that are necessary for getting the fullest exposure from their software.

2. Make sure that each MP3 file has information included in its ID3 tags. These metadata fields are designed to describe music files, but the library can insert its own information in the fields for artist, album, song, etc. In addition, comments fields can be used to add URLs, contact information, and e-mail addresses.

3. Create a graphic or logo for the podcast to be added to the ID3 tag for album art. Providence Public Library has developed simple yet effective graphic images to brand their podcasts. If creating videocasts, libraries can insert graphics at the start or end of each episode. The Westerville Public Library ends each of its videocasts with white type on a black screen proclaiming: "Westerville Public Library. Delivering the Future."

4. Make clear at the start of each episode who and what is being presented. Failing to do so risks disorienting the listener. Kankakee Public Library includes an introduction at the start of every episode describing what is to follow. Also, identifying each speaker on an episode is a valuable way to personalize the library and enable feedback.

A Note on Podfading

Podfading refers to the act of discontinuing a podcast, whether through lack of resources, interest, or burnout. It is not uncommon for people to experiment with podcasting and, after a number of episodes, decide that the process is too time con-suming to continue (Friess 2006). The podcasts simply fade away.

The implication for libraries is an important one. If listeners are used to the prevalent model of radio-like podcasts, with regularly scheduled episodes, the library's commit-ment to produce is not to be taken lightly. Although many libraries have experimented with podcasting, it remains to be seen if they will continue on a consistent basis.

Also, the roles of those involved should be well defined and distributed. The time commitment attached to podcasting is high and the danger of burnout real if not enough people are involved and invested in its success.

GETTING STARTED

The technical and monetary investment in starting a podcast is quite low. Using existing computers, open source programs, and low-cost recording equipment, a library can have the technical details of a podcast taken care of in a day. While many complete guides to podcasting are available, the basic equipment needed is as follows:

Microphones

Low-cost microphones are readily available from electronics and computer stores. For podcasts involving only one person speaking, headset microphones or simple desktop models will suffice. Upgrading the microphone, however, is the surest way to improve audio quality.

Recording a live event is more complicated. Digital audio recorders can be used if the sound system is not capable of capturing a recording itself. Careful attention needs to be paid to the placement of the microphone to ensure that all speakers can be heard.

Recording/Editing Software

The recording can be done directly to a desktop or laptop computer running sound editing software. How heavily a podcast is to be edited is an individual decision, based on time, skill, and level of quality desired.

The RSS Feed

RSS feeds are simple text files written in XML. They can be created by hand following any number of existing templates or modified from an existing podcast's feed. If podcasts are being posted to a blog, as many libraries are doing, the blog software can often create the RSS feed. There are also free online services that can be used to create podcast feeds.

Hosting Files

The audio files can be hosted on the library's own servers or, if space is an issue, there are online services that can be used. Hosted services can offer fairly detailed statistics gathering which will aid in assessment.

LOOKING AHEAD

If more libraries become content creators, providing access to programming on a regular basis, how does that shift the role of the library? It opens up a unique and interesting possibility for the institution. How wide an audience could library programming attract, with its vast array of author talks, scholarly lectures, and practical workshops on everything from genealogy to dog training? Is there a place for the library as its own network? The Lifelong Learning Channel?

One development that would help explore this possibility would be the creation of a robust, independently maintained library podcast directory on par with iTunes.[6] With enough content made easily accessible and with support of the tagging functionality of sites such as Flickr and del.icio.us to allow users and librarians to create subject terms and group the content in different ways, such a directory could prove effective in drawing attention and support to library podcasts. With the proper promotion and partnerships, the day may come when a search for a book in Amazon.com will link to a podcast from a public library featuring a reading by the author.

Until that day, librarians see enough possibilities in podcasting to keep the exploration going. Now that institutions have become familiar with the technology, more work will need to be done to assess the usefulness of podcasting, establish best practices, and develop resources and training. As podcasting continues to evolve as a means of communication and education, libraries will continue to find ways to include it in their mission.

NOTES

1. Alternative terms suggested by Hammersley in the same article included audioblogging and guerilla media.

2. The response to the Pew Report on podcasting highlights the early difficulties in accurately tracking and defining statistics on podcasting. Many questioned the survey's use of the phrase "radio internet program" alongside podcasting in its instrument.

3. Library bloggers who created podcasts or individual audioblog posts during the early months of 2005 include Greg Schwartz (Open Stacks), Karen Schneider (Free Range Librarian), and Michael Stephens (Tame the Web). Dave King (Dave's Blog) also created a videocast.

4. "Podcast" was the *New Oxford American Dictionary*'s Word of the Year for 2005. Other contenders were "bird flu" and "persistent vegetative state."

5. Although the most common example of a podcast is an audio file in MP3 format, there are a number of file types that can be delivered in this way, including images, video, PDFs, and PowerPoint presentations.

6. Two websites that are attempting to create such a directory are LISPods at http://lispodcasts.com/ and LibraryPods at http://librarypods.com/.

REFERENCES

Balas, J. "Blogging is so last year: Now podcasting is hot." *Computers in Libraries* 25, no. 10 (2005): 29–32.

Campbell, G. "There's something in the air: Podcasting in education." *EDUCAUSE Review* 40, no. 6 (2005): 32–47.

The Diffusion Group. "Podcasting users to approach 60 million US consumers by 2010." June 15, 2005. http://www.tdgresearch.com/press044.htm (retrieved October 5, 2006).

EDUCAUSE Learning Initiative. "7 things you should know about Podcasting." June 2005. http://www.educause.edu/ir/library/pdf/ELI7003.pdf (retrieved October 5, 2006).

Farivar, C. "New food for iPods: Audio by subscription." *New York Times*, October 28, 2004, p. G5.

Friess, S. "Podfading takes its toll." *Wired News*, February 7, 2006. http://www.wired.com/news/technology/070171-0.html (retrieved October 3, 2006).

Hammersley, B. "Audible revolution." *The Guardian*, February 12, 2004. http://arts.guardian.co.uk/features/story/0,1145758,00.html (retrieved October 10, 2006).

Kennedy, R. "With irreverence and an iPod, recreating the museum tour." *New York Times*, May 28, 2005, p. A1.

Rainie, L. and M. Madden. "Podcasting catches on." *Pew Internet & American Life Project*, April 2005. http://www.pewinternet.org/PPF/r/154/report_display.asp (retrieved September 12, 2006).

Stephens, M. "Do libraries matter: On library & librarian 2.0." [weblog entry] *ALA TechSource*, November 18, 2005. http://www.techsource.ala.org/blog/2005/11/do-libraries-matter-on-library-librarian-20.html (retrieved October 10, 2006).

FURTHER READINGS

EDUCAUSE Resource Center for Podcasting. http://www.educause.edu/Browse/645?PARENT_ID=788 (retrieved November 1, 2006).

Goeghegan, M. W. and D. Flas. *Podcasting solutions: The complete guide to podcasting.* Berkeley, CA: Apress, 2005.

Gordon-Murnane, L. "Saying 'I Do' to podcasting." *Searcher: The magazine for database professionals* 13, no. 6 (2005): 44–51.

Podcasting and iTunes: Technical specifications. http://www.apple.com/itunes/store/podcaststechspecs.html (retrieved November 1, 2006).

Podcasting News. http://www.podcastingnews.com/ (retrieved September 8, 2006).

Podsafe Music Network. http://music.podshow.com/ (retrieved November 3, 2006).

Vogele, C., M. Garlick, and the Berkman Center Clinical Program in Cyberlaw. *Podcasting Legal Guide.* http://wiki.creativecommons.org/Podcasting_Legal_Guide (retrieved October 10, 2006).

Walch, R. and M. Lafferty. *Tricks of the podcasting masters.* Indianapolis, IN: QUE Publishing, 2006.

RESOURCES

The following are resources that can be used for finding, creating, and managing podcasts.

Directories

Education Podcast Network: http://epnweb.org/
iTunes: http://www.apple.com/itunes/
Podcast Alley: http://www.podcastalley.com/

Feed Generators

ListGarden: http://softwaregarden.com/products/listgarden/
PodcastBlaster: http://www.podcastblaster.com/podcast-feed/
FeedForAll: http://www.feedforall.com/index.htm

Hosting Services

LibSyn: https://www.libsyn.com/
Odeo: http://odeo.com/
Ourmedia: http://www.ourmedia.org/

Listener Feedback Services

K7: http://www.k7.net/
MobaTalk (web-based): http://www.mobatalk.com/

Podcatchers

Fireant (for videocasts): http://getfireant.com/
iTunes: http://www.apple.com/itunes/
Juice: http://juicereceiver.sourceforge.net/index.php

Podsafe Music

ccMixter: http://www.ccmixter.org/
IODA PROMONET: http://promonet.iodalliance.com/login.php
Podsafe Music Network: http://music.podshow.com/

Sound Recording/Editing Programs

Adobe Audition: http://www.adobe.com/products/audition/
Audacity: http://audacity.sourceforge.net/
GarageBand (Mac): http://www.apple.com/ilife/garageband/

Video Editing

Final Cut Pro (Mac): http://www.apple.com/finalcutstudio/finalcutpro/
Windows Movie Maker: http://www.microsoft.com/windowsxp/downloads/updates/
moviemaker2.mspx

5

HANDHELD COMPUTERS IN LIBRARIES

Christopher Strauber

The first computers were impersonal, imposing, and very, very large. Each generation of computers has become smaller, more powerful, more personal, and more widely used. The current generation of handheld computers is small enough to be truly portable, powerful enough to rival desktop PCs of a few years ago, and inexpensive enough to be within the reach of ordinary consumers. They range in complexity from devices that do only one or two things to computers that can play music or video, surf the web, send and receive e-mail, work with spreadsheets or documents, keep track of databases, connect wirelessly to the Internet via home and office networks, etc. The most complex devices are also the most expensive. But for $100 a Palm Z22 PDA will do most of those things, and a Motorola Q smart phone all of them.

This chapter will discuss what handheld computers are and what they can do for libraries and their patrons. It will briefly describe a rather lengthy list of devices with possible library applications, then outline their current and possible future uses as means of communication, access to media (audio, video, or text), and access to the web. It will also make suggestions for further reading and trend spotting.

THE DEVICES

For purposes of this discussion I will define "handheld computer" as any device weighing less than 2 pounds that is capable of performing one or more of the library-relevant functions of a computer. This covers a surprisingly broad range of devices.

The consumer electronics marketplace is a moving target. New products arrive daily and old products quickly change to suit the latest fashion, or simply disappear. The first Apple iPod was released on October 23, 2001. As of December 2006 there have been six major versions of the full-sized iPod, the iPod Mini, two versions of the iPod nano, and two versions of the iPod shuffle. The rest of the consumer electronics industry has released hundreds of competing devices, all attempting to unseat Apple by some combination of clever marketing, extra features, price, style, or whimsy. Each category of handhelds has a similar story.

This survey of major device types and their functions is designed to provide an overview only. Reviews at websites such as Engadget (www.engadget. com) or CNET (www.cnet. com) provide in-depth reviews, pictures, and often video of the devices in use. Many of these devices are also on display at major electronics retailers.

MP3 Players

Price range: $50–$500. Examples: Apple iPod, Creative Zen V, Samsung YP-U2

MP3 players play music; some display pictures, text, or video files as well. The name comes from the MP3 file format all of them have in common. They come in all shapes, sizes, and price ranges. Even the smallest can store hundreds of songs; the largest have as much storage as most desktop computers. Because they are, in essence, large disk drives most players can also serve as portable storage devices for files from the user's computer or other computers.

Portable Media Players

Price range: $200–$700. Examples: Cowon A2, Archos 504

Portable Media Players, or PMPs, are designed for portable video, but typically also include the features of MP3 players. They have larger screens, larger storage capacities, and usually a larger price as well. Some PMPs can serve as portable video recorders.

Ebook Readers

Price range: $100–$700. Examples: Sony Reader, iRex iLiad, Rocket eBook Pro

Most handhelds can read ebooks; these were purpose-built to do it. The Rocket ebook reader is an example from the last generation of products designed to deliver book length texts in digital form. The Sony Reader and iRex iLiad are examples from the newest generation of these devices, which attempt to address the problem of screen resolution with new technology. A printed page has a resolution of about 300 dots per inch; a typical computer or personal digital assistant (PDA) has about 80 dpi resolution. The new screen technology is comparable to newsprint, approximately 150 dpi. The Sony and iRex devices, still not in mass distribution in the United States as this chapter is being written, will also have the ability to display pictures and play audio files.

Portable Gaming Devices

Price range: $150–$200. Examples: Nintendo DS Lite, Sony PSP

These are designed to play video games, but other useful features are creeping in. Both examples include support for wireless game play. Current models support limited web browsers. The Sony PSP was also designed to be a media player, with support for audio and video playback.

Cell Phones and Feature Phones

Price range: $0 (sometimes, with service contract)–$700 Examples: Nokia 6215i, LG Chocolate

Cell phones are the most common form of handheld computer. The simplest are merely portable wireless telephones. Feature phones add digital cameras, music players, simple web and/or e-mail access, navigation systems, games, calculators, and an assortment of other services.

PDAs

Price range: $100–$500. Examples: Palm TX, Dell Axim X51

Personal Digital Assistants are the classic handheld computer. The simplest are digital versions of a day planner and address book; the most complex are full-fledged computers, equivalent in processing power to desktop computers from a few years ago. Mid-range devices, like the Palm TX, have relatively large screens and wireless Internet access. They can play audio and video files, read ebooks, and view or edit documents in most common formats. They can, with the proper software, perform almost any function of a standard computer, limited only by the size of the screen and the stylus as input.

Smart Phones

Price range: $100–$500. Examples: Treo 700p, Motorola Q, Nokia E62

Smart phones combine the features of cell phones with those of PDAs.

Internet Tablets

Price range: $300–$800. Examples: Nokia 770, Sony Mylo

Internet tablets like the Nokia 770 and Sony Mylo are designed to provide the basics of the web in portable form: browsing, text-messaging and chat, and voice communication through services such as Google Talk and Skype. Both devices can also serve as portable music players or text readers, but have relatively limited storage capacities.

UMPCs

Price range: $1000–$2000. Examples: Samsung Q1, Kohjisha SA1F00

Ultra Mobile PCs are a new class of device recently introduced in an attempt to put a full desktop computer operating system into something the size of a large PDA. These expensive devices include Windows XP, wireless, and substantial memory and storage capacity. Judging by reviews, there are some kinks to be worked out in the first generation of these devices, but the idea has considerable promise. The Kohjisha model includes a 7-inch screen and a nearly full-sized keyboard that fold together into a package that weighs just over 2 pounds.

Table 5.1
Handheld computers, main features

Device	Input type	Screen size	Communication (voice, text, e-mail)	Wireless web	Media (audio, video, text)
MP3 player	None	Up to 3"	None	None	Audio, text
Portable media player	None	3–7"	None	None	All
Ebook reader	None or stylus	Up to 7"	None	Some	Text, audio
Portable gaming device	Stylus or buttons	3–4"	All	Yes (limited)	All
Cell phone	Number pad or thumb keyboard	Varies	Voice, SMS, some e-mail	Yes (limited)	Text
PDA	Stylus	3–4"	All	Yes	All
Smart phone	Varies	2–3"	All	Yes	All
Internet tablet	Stylus or thumb keyboard	2–4"	All	Yes	All
UMPC	Thumb keyboard	4–7"	All	Yes	All
Tablet PC	Stylus and full keyboard	12–14"	All	Yes	All

Tablet PCs

Price range: $1500–$2500. Examples: Lenovo Thinkpad X41, Toshiba Portege

The current generation of tablet PCs are essentially laptop computers with the option to use a stylus rather than a keyboard and mouse for input. Some have rotating screens. They tend to be more expensive than similarly featured laptops, but are very popular in some industries. The smallest of these just barely fit into the handheld category as defined here.

This is a long list of devices, but their functions are similar. Table 5.1 lists the devices in terms of the three main areas mentioned in the introduction: communication, access to media, and access to the web. Those functions, rather than the particular devices, are the things for libraries to watch. Screen sizes are included to give a sense of the scale of the device.

The variety of devices available allows customers to choose the appropriate combination of price, size, and range of functions to suit their needs. For example, with the exception of the most basic cell phones, almost any device discussed so far could be used to listen to music or podcasts. A small MP3 player would probably be the smallest and most economical choice, though that would assume a desktop or laptop computer with an Internet connection to download the files. That computer could itself be used as a player, but it would be difficult to fit into a shirt pocket. Someone wanting to listen to podcasts and to chat and e-mail on one smallish wireless device could choose an Internet tablet, PDA, or smart phone. In this case the audio content could be saved to the device's memory and used anywhere, but e-mail and chat would be dependent on the wireless or cellular networks available. Choices about which device is the appropriate one will inevitably be very personal, and therefore hard to predict.

One other relatively obvious point is that many of these devices are expensive and, in the case of smart phones with mobile data plans, expensive to maintain. MP3 players have dropped in price to the point that low-end models are about the same price as low-end portable CD players, but the MP3 player requires access to a computer to work. In making purchasing and collection development decisions we should remember that, to borrow a phrase from science fiction author William Gibson, the future is here, but it is unevenly distributed.

This variety of products and the nature of the marketplace have two important implications for library services. First, it is likely that patrons will have and use a wide variety of devices, some old and some new. Second, it will be impossible for any library to support all of them. How, then, should libraries choose which devices to support?

A rough and ready rule of thumb might be that supporting any technology most of your patrons have is probably a good idea. According to U.S. government statistics, in 2003 about 96 percent of American households owned a telephone, 98 percent a television, 62 percent had a computer, and 54 percent had Internet access. In 1980 that number for VCRs was 1.1 percent. By 1990 it was 68 percent (U.S. Census Bureau 2005, 737), by which point most libraries had added video tapes to their collections. Telephone ownership passed 50 percent of households in 1946 (U.S. Census Bureau 1975, 783). The 1957 movie *Desk Set* concerns a telephone reference service which appears to be threatened with replacement by computers, which indicates both that telephone reference service was familiar enough then to make a good movie plot, and, somewhat more to the point, that changing technology is not a new problem. The pattern would seem to be library support when ownership reaches 50 percent of households.

Mobile computing is quickly becoming that widespread. A 2005 consumer electronics industry report indicated that 81 percent of households owned DVD players, 78 percent owned cell phones, 34 percent owned notebook computers, and 25 percent owned MP3 players ("MP3 Players, Digital Cameras" 2006). The percentages for notebook computers and MP3 players are below the threshold, but rising quickly, particularly for MP3 players, whose sales tripled in a year. Cell phones are already more widely owned than computers. The trend is clearly toward more and more functions moving into smaller and smaller devices. One estimate has 100 million music-equipped phones sold worldwide this year, with 800 million by 2010 ("Microsoft, Nokia" 2006), and smart phone sales were projected to be 120 million this year ("Mobile phone sales" 2006). These numbers are too big to ignore.

Another important consideration for libraries, in addition to aggregate numbers like these, is the composition of each library's particular group of patrons. Apple computers have about a 5 percent market share, with over 90 percent Windows. But Apple's share is about 11 percent of notebook computers, and their general market share is much higher among educators, artists, musicians, and graphic designers. Smart phones and BlackBerries are not as widely popular as MP3 players, but PDA or smart phone adoption among doctors is very high, 30–50 percent, and is even higher among medical students, 80 percent (Tenopir 2004). Lawyers, government officials, and business travelers are also likely early adopters.

COMMUNICATION

Reference service by telephone is not new, but the ubiquity of cell phones puts that service in almost everyone's pocket. Voice over IP or VOIP services allow a computer to serve as a telephone. Skype is one popular service, but there are many others, including the voice services associated with Yahoo! and AOL's instant messaging services. Computer to computer calls are free, and calls to regular phones are cheap and largely ignore distance. Because it can work over a wired or wireless Internet connection it offers the possibility of pushing phone access into spaces where no cellular signal or telephone cord will reach, useful for librarians in the depths of the stacks. PDAs and Internet tablets often support this, as do tablet PCs and UMPCs. Cell phones, for obvious reasons, typically do not, though T-Mobile is currently experimenting with it.

E-mail remains the web's most important function for most people. A study estimated that almost 22 billion nonspam e-mail messages were sent daily in 2004, with projections for these numbers to increase dramatically over the next five years (OCLC 2004). It is apparently a major factor in smart phone sales ("FYI" 2006). It is also one of the most widely supported functions: cell phones, PDAs, Internet tablets, UMPCs, and tablet PCs all support it. Even MP3 players like the iPod, which can read simple text files, can be used to read, but not write, e-mail.

E-mail on small devices is, barring occasional problems with handling attachments, very similar to e-mail on all kinds of computers. Text is text. Some devices have trouble managing e-mail with attachments, but PDAs and smart phones designed for business users as a rule include the ability to open and/or edit Microsoft Office documents and at least some audio or video formats. However, devices without keyboards severely limit the length of messages most people are willing or able to send.

Instant messaging, also known as IM or chat, is a somewhat more complicated issue. The devices do not necessarily support all IM services, and users have their own preferred services in any event. This implies that libraries planning to offer chat reference services should maintain accounts on as many services as possible. This can be easier than it sounds, as programs, such as Gaim, Trillian, and Adium, or the web-based Meebo, allow one librarian to monitor half a dozen chat services at once.

Text messages are another potentially relevant channel for patron-librarian communication. OCLC (2004) estimated 2 billion Short Message Service or SMS messages daily in 2004. The 150- to 200-character limit of SMS text messages is a serious limitation, but the mobile version of Google Answers indicates that there is some demand for questions in this form.

Traditional reference service, with fixed service points, is partly driven by technology. Proximity to the print reference collection is obviously still relevant, but portable computers and portable telephones make it possible to seek patrons at their point of need rather than forcing them to come to us at our point of convenience—while still being available to remote users by phone, e-mail, or chat. Patrons will have a variety of devices with a variety of functions, but librarians can arrange to have devices that provide access to phone, chat, e-mail, and the Internet, either via handheld or desktop computers.

DIGITAL MEDIA, DIGITAL RIGHTS

Digital distribution is a two-edged sword for media companies. Reducing costs related to production and marketing is one edge, the ease of digital piracy the other. Most major content providers, with a few notable exceptions like eMusic and Magnatune, have opted to distribute their products with software and/or hardware designed to ensure that their intellectual property rights are respected. The technology is collectively referred to as Digital Rights Management or DRM. It affects almost all aspects of handheld computing.

DRM typically restricts what one can do with a particular file. Some DRM-protected files can be burned to CD or DVD, some cannot. Some can be copied to other computers or devices, usually a limited number; some cannot. Frequently the DRM is associated with a particular media player and can only be played using that software, or only using a particular device. From the publishers' perspective it is not a problem if users have to repurchase their entire music collection should they decide they want to try a different MP3 player; many users disagree. Copyright law has always said that copying a substantial portion of a piece of copyrighted material is infringement, but traditional media like books, tapes, and CDs have no self-enforcement mechanism. Media companies are using new technology to assert their rights with varying degrees of vigor.

The challenge for libraries is that digital files are less flexible than what they replace. A CD purchased anywhere will play on any device that plays CDs. Digital music purchased online typically works on only one type of device, either the iPod or Windows Media Player devices. Digital movies, at least at the moment, often cannot be played except on a computer. Ebooks cannot be resold or traded.

An irony is that DRM is typically not difficult to remove or circumvent. People who are determined to break the law can usually do so quite easily. This is not to condone piracy, merely to point out that DRM chiefly inconveniences paying customers.

Ebooks

Ebooks have many theoretical advantages. They weigh nothing, take up no physical space, and occupy very little disk space. A plain text version of *War and Peace* is roughly the same size as a single song in MP3 format; most handhelds can hold hundreds of them with no additional memory added. Most ebook formats are searchable, which is incredibly useful for reference works like dictionaries. Ebooks can make tables of contents and indexes work like hyperlinks. There is a wide variety of content available, both freely available and commercial.

Of the freely available content, Project Gutenberg is the largest and oldest. It contains about 19,000 public domain works laboriously and mostly manually typed and proofread by volunteers. Because Project Gutenberg texts are public domain and can be freely redistributed, other sites and services have sprung up around it. One, Manybooks.net, reformats a collection of mostly Gutenberg-derived texts into a variety of e-reader formats. The University of Pennsylvania's Online Books page provides a search engine, but also a list arranged by Library of Congress call numbers.

There is a variety of commercial content. Major players like Mobipocket, eReader, and the Palm eBook Store, among others, offer a fairly broad range of titles, including the full range of standard bookstore fare, from bestsellers to cookbooks to self-help. Sony, hoping to recreate the iTunes-iPod ecosystem, has opened Sony Connect, a similar store, to provide titles for its new Reader. Each store has reader software associated with it.

Despite many predictions of the printed book's imminent demise, ebook sales remain minuscule (Crawford 2006). The reasons typically listed are: small, low-resolution screens on ebook readers; an aversion to reading long-form content on screens, which may be tied to physiology and psychology (Garland and Noyes 2004); and the bewildering array of mutually incompatible formats and DRM schemes that are available.

There are some promising developments, however, which may help alleviate some of these problems, two relating to technology and two to format.

Display technology is improving. The new readers by Sony and iRex address one of the major factors cited by Garland and Noyes by improving the resolution and creating a screen that does not flicker. The International Digital Publishing Forum recently published an open ebook standard, which the major players in ebooks, including Adobe, Mobipocket, eReader, and others, have said they will support ("OCF 1.0 Released" 2006).

There is a strong market for reference books in electronic form. Miller (2005) describes several solutions for business and IT, including Safari, which provides access to computer manuals and training materials published by O'Reilly and others. Cuddy (2005) outlines the wealth of standard reference works available in ebook form for law, medicine, and the humanities. Library subscription services such as Literature Resource Center, Oxford Reference Online, and Xrefer offer the same service to a slightly different audience. Reference books by definition are not read at length, which fits well with the 8 minutes' average use reported by a NetLibrary representative (Harrison 2006). Crawford (2006) suggests that ebooks should focus on areas where they can do something better than print. This is one such area.

Another approach is exemplified by Harlequin On The Go and Daily Lit. These services serialize full-length books. Harlequin provides serial access to hundreds of romance titles as an add-on to Verizon cell phone service. Daily Lit (www.dailylit.com), a free service, takes books in the public domain, breaks them up into thousand word chunks, and sends them by e-mail to subscribers. This addresses the long document problem by creating shorter documents.

Music

The legal music download market is dominated by Apple, the iPod, and the iTunes Store, which account for 80 percent of sales of digital music and about 70 percent of U.S. sales of MP3 players. Apple sells songs for 99 cents and albums for $9.99. The store also sells audio books, television programs, and movies, some exclusive to Apple and iTunes. In the 3 years since the store began selling music, over 1 billion songs have been sold worldwide. In order to use the music store users must download Apple's iTunes software, which organizes the user's music and podcast collection and manages the necessary digital rights. The software will also synchronize the computer's music collection with one or more iPods.

Apple's competitors, including Napster, Rhapsody, Yahoo! Music, and others, offer a set of similar services: downloads, a software program for rights management and organization, synchronization with portable music players, and a large music library to choose from. Most of them use Windows Media DRM, which works with a wide variety of MP3 players instead of just one. Second, a Windows Media-based DRM scheme called PlaysForSure allows a different way of getting access to music, namely subscription. For a monthly fee, a rather large list of approved devices can download and play any song in the music store's collection. Copying or sharing downloaded songs is usually strictly controlled if not outright prohibited. As long as the fee is paid every month users get the benefit of a vast collection; but when the service is cancelled the files are locked and useless. Neither approach has so far proven successful enough to threaten Apple's share of the commercial market, as the second-ranked digital music vendor is eMusic, which offers DRM-free music from mostly independent artists, at 11 percent (Graham 2006).

A subscription model is apparently not what users expect when they go shopping on the web. However, it is exactly like the model currently used by libraries to lend physical media. Overdrive, an Ohio-based company, has created a service now in use by many libraries to create a similar library of digital media, including music, audio books, ebooks, and film, and make it available by a subscription corresponding to the library's loan period. Participating libraries include the New York Public Library, the Cleveland Public Library, and many others.

The complexity is the DRM. It is Windows Media, but specifically a variety of Windows Media that requires a Windows computer. This excludes Macintosh users, but more importantly, iPod users. Overdrive's software allows CD burning, so there is a rather obvious way to move the content from the Windows Media format to one an iPod can read but it is time consuming and likely violates the Digital Millennium Copyright Act, not to mention the licensing terms. Also, each medium requires a separate player to be downloaded and installed on the patron's computer. The system works, but the sheer volume of written instructions provided by the Cleveland Public Library (2006) says something about how easy it is to use. This is in no way intended to criticize Overdrive's service, which is very popular and, more importantly, the first attempt to create for library users something like what is currently available for individuals on the web. Overdrive is as easy to use as the law and current technology allow.

Video

Digital video is probably the most challenging of the three main formats for library purposes. There is a welter of incomprehensible file formats; most players only handle a few of them; and portable video players tend to be the most expensive of the media devices.

Apple's iTunes store began selling downloads of television programs in October 2005, and has sold millions in the year since (Datamonitor 2006, 19). Apple began to sell full-length movies in the fall of 2006, as did Amazon.com's Unbox service;

Microsoft announced a rental service would be available through Xbox Live. There are also a variety of other commercial websites such as CinemaNow and Movielink that offer movies for purchase or rental. For the most part these services allow the movies downloaded to be played only on the computer that downloaded them, which is a pretty severe limitation. One other difficulty is that downloading a file the size of a DVD can take an hour or more over even a fast Internet connection. Despite these restrictions, Disney reports that half a million movies were sold through iTunes in the first two months they were available (Cheng 2006).

Live television is becoming mobile as well. Devices like the Slingbox and programs like MobiTV allow television programs to be streamed via wireless Internet to handhelds. The classic user example is of the traveling salesman who wants to follow his hometown football team. Wherever he is he can connect to his home network and watch, on his mobile device, the television programs he could watch at home. VCRs are familiar technology. Their replacements, digital video recorders like the TiVo, can take video recorded at home and make it viewable on handhelds.

The YouTube phenomenon, and its implications for libraries and the future of television and other media, deserves a separate article. YouTube is a video-sharing website that allows users to upload video they have recorded. The site then translates the video into a form that almost anyone with a web browser can view and makes it available for comment, linking, and display on the user's own website. The simplicity and popularity of it have, within a year, translated into millions of downloads per day and a $1.65 billion buyout by Google. There is already software that can turn YouTube video into files readable by handhelds, but the more advanced web browsers on UMPCs, tablets, and some smart phones and PDAs can view them on the web.

NEW MEDIA AND THE LIBRARY

Libraries have traditionally collected a variety of materials in a variety of formats, but for the most part they have collected materials produced by commercial publishers. Libraries have not traditionally collected radio shows, because unless a broadcast is recorded there is nothing to put in the collection. Podcasts and web video by definition produce something collectible, and there are tens of thousands of them. Many are ephemeral; but others are simply a different format for the sorts of things libraries collect already: entertainment, news, and information for all sorts of audiences. The move toward user-generated content that is affecting traditional media outlets also affects libraries which are, among other things, storehouses of traditional media. It is tempting to take the long view and wait to see what develops over time. We do not have that luxury. A gaffe publicized by a YouTube video is widely accounted to have played an important part in the narrow defeat of Virginia senator George Allen in the 2006 election (Lizza 2006; "Allen defeat" 2006). Who will preserve that video, and make it available for future researchers? If not librarians, who?

THE WIRELESS WEB

The web is the delivery system and display mechanism for almost everything related to libraries and Web 2.0. Handheld computers with wireless access mean the library and its services can be anywhere and everywhere, provided the necessary steps to support portable computing are taken.

The major limitations of handheld computers for web access are: limited screen size and resolution, varying browser capabilities, varying access speeds, and inefficient tools for data entry. Screen sizes range from small to very small. Web browsers may or may not be able to handle complex web pages and interactivity. Speeds range from slow dial-up speed to broadband speeds. Patrons may be spelling out words using the keypad on their cell phones, writing on screen with a stylus, or pecking away at a thumb keyboard, and will likely consider anything more than a few words as a long document.

Creating a good user experience for mobile users may require some website redesign. Cuddy (2006) summarizes the design specifics: offer the content patrons are most likely to want; be concise; don't use large graphics for navigation or to provide critical information; limit the amount of text input required. As Cuddy (2006) and Fox (2003) point out, these are not terribly different from the guidelines for creating websites for users with disabilities, which many libraries have already done. Also, the similar guidelines for websites designed for lower literacy users tend to result in websites easier for everyone to use (Nielsen 2005). Simpler is better.

This raises an interesting existential question. Can the range of services offered by the library's website be reduced to an essential core that can be effectively displayed on a 2-inch screen? If it can, those core features should be the focus of the main website as well. Creating simple interfaces and websites that do a few things very well is one of the hallmarks of Web 2.0.

A wide variety of websites and services have been optimized for mobile devices. Newspapers like the *Christian Science Monitor* and *Washington Post* have mobile-optimized versions. Google Mobile and Yahoo! Mobile offer a reasonable subset of their services, including search. Major library subscription services do the same, particularly in medicine and law. Ovid@Hand and PubMed On Tap offer alerts and a simplified search interface (Tenopir 2004). Westlaw has a wireless version and Lexis-Nexis offers a service designed for BlackBerries. ILS vendors SirsiDynix and Innovative sell mobile-optimized versions of their OPAC interfaces. These are the distinctive tools of libraries, and making them work in this way is the first step to putting the library in everyone's pocket.

CONCLUSIONS AND SUGGESTIONS

Handheld computers will continue to come in an endless variety of shapes and sizes, but by focusing on function rather than form libraries can provide services and collections that reach out to where our patrons are.

Support the technology your patrons have. Cell phones are more common than computers, and libraries can better support their capacity for voice, text, and e-mail communication by slightly expanding existing services. The digital divide is real, but it is smaller where cell phones are concerned. Support the wireless web. This may require a little more effort, but the process of deciding on the simplest possible way to display the essence of your library's services will benefit all of your patrons, not just handheld users. Make your content available in the formats your patrons are using, and accept that digital books may come in many forms and serve different purposes.

This will go a long way toward supporting all the devices described here, many that are not, and some of the ones that will be introduced 10 minutes after you read this.

SOURCES FOR MORE INFORMATION AND TREND SPOTTING

Libraries, particularly medical libraries, have been early adopters of mobile computing technology. For more detail on library-specific handheld information, consult Megan Fox's excellent list of resources (2006). For more detail on the devices themselves, go to the web. Try sites like CNET or Engadget. Podcasts such as CNET's Buzz Out Loud (Merritt, Wood, and Belmont 2006) and This Week in Tech (Laporte et al. 2006) cover the tech industry generally, with good gadget coverage. The Engadget podcast (Rojas and Block 2006) is more focused. All are done by industry professionals with style, wit, and a user-centered focus.

REFERENCES

"Allen defeat seals Senate swing." *St. Petersburg Times*, November 10, 2006, p. 15 A.

Cheng, J. *Disney nears half-million sales through iTunes*. 2006. http://arstechnica.com/news.ars/post/20061110-8198.html (accessed November 10, 2006).

Cleveland Public Library. *Help*. 2006. http://dlc.clevnet.org/11B564F3-5C81-4288-85D7-E7A650FB2E4B/10/210/en/Help.htm (accessed November 14, 2006).

Crawford, W. "Why aren't ebooks more successful?" *Econtent* 29, no. 8 (2006): 44.

Cuddy, C. *Using PDAs in libraries: A how-to-do-it manual*. New York: Neal-Schuman, 2005.

———. "How to serve content to PDA users on-the-go." *Computers in Libraries* 26, no. 4 (2006): 10–15.

Datamonitor. *Apple Computer, Inc*. 2006. Accessed on November 14, 2006, from Business Source Premier.

Fox, M. K. "A library in your palm." *Library Journal* 128, no. 3 (2003): 10–15.

———. *PDAs, handhelds and mobile technologies in libraries*. 2006. http://web.simmons.edu/~fox/pda (accessed November 14, 2006).

"FYI." *Network Computing* 17, no. 20 (2006): 20.

Garland, K. J. and P. M. Noyes. "CRT monitors: do they interfere with learning?" *Behaviour and Information Technology* 23, no. 1 (2004): 43–52.

Graham, J. "EMusic's pitch: Download song and own it." *USA Today.com*, July 30, 2006. http://www.usatoday.com/tech/products/services/2006-07-30-emusic_x.htm (accessed November 10, 2006).

Harrison, G. "Audiobook 3.0: the convergence of the mobile lifestyle platform." Presentation at ALA Annual Conference, New Orleans, June 28, 2006.

Laporte, L. et al. *This week in tech*. [podcast]. 2006.http://www.twit.tv/TWiT (accessed November 14, 2006).

Lizza, R. "The YouTube Election." *New York Times*, August 20, 2006, p. 1.

Merritt, T., M. Wood, and V. Belmont. *Buzz out loud: CNET's podcast ofindeterminate length*. 2006. http://reviews.cnet.com/4520-11455_7-6457370-1.html (accessed November 14, 2006).

"Microsoft, Nokia have work cut out to rival iPod." [Electronic version]. *eWeek*, September 6, 2006, n.p. Accessed on November 15, 2006, from Infotrac Onefile.

Miller, R. "Ebooks worm their way into the reference market." *Econtent* (July/August 2005): 30–34.

"Mobile phone sales grow 21% in 2005." *Electronic News* 52, no. 10 (2006): 25.

"MP3 players, digital cameras lead household CE growth." *Electronic News* 52, no. 15 (2006): 11.

Nielsen, J. *Lower-literacy users.* 2005. http://www.useit.com/alertbox/20050314.html (accessed November 14, 2006).

International Digital Publishing Forum. *OCF 1.0 released.* 2006. http://www.idpf.org/pressroom/pressreleases/ocf1.0.htm (accessed November 13, 2006).

OCLC. *2004 information format trends: content, not containers.* 2004. http://www.oclc.org/reports/2004format.htm (accessed November 14, 2006).

Rojas, P. and R. Block. *Engadget podcast.* 2006. http://www.engadget.com/category/podcasts/ (accessed November 14, 2006).

Tenopir, C. "Searching on the run." *Library Journal* 129, no. 16 (2004): 32.

U.S. Census Bureau. *Statistical abstract of the United States.* Washington, DC: Government Printing Office, 2005, Table 1117, p. 737.

U.S. Census Bureau. *Historical statistics of the United States, colonial times to 1970, bicentennial edition.* Washington, DC: Government Printing Office, 1975, Part 2, Series R 1=12, p. 783.

6

MASHUPS AND WEB SERVICES

Eric Schnell

The web has been built using relatively simple technologies that have proven to have sufficient scalability, efficiency, and utility. This simplistic architecture has resulted in an amazing information space of interrelated resources that connect people across cultures, languages, and media. Functionality traditionally installed and run on a local computer in a single application is now performed on the network involving many applications running on many computers. The web is becoming the operating system to which developers are creating reusable, constantly updated software components that are delivered over the Internet and that can be embedded or loosely coupled with other web applications. The *mashup* represents the first generation of this type of web-based applications.

Mashups are revolutionizing application development in an era of the participatory and interactive web in the same way that blogging has revolutionized online publishing. The ease of repurposing web content and the availability of technologies and tools to develop applications based on this content have been the driving factors for the popularity of mashups. Much as the open access movement is creating opportunities that are reshaping the structure of scholarly communications, the web mashup also creates new opportunities to reshape library information systems.

This chapter will introduce and discuss the concepts and technologies associated with and used in the creation of a web mashup application. Possible roles for the mashup in libraries will be discussed and a few practical library-oriented applications will be highlighted and described. As one may anticipate, there are many acronyms, development platforms, and protocols that are associated with this technology. These building blocks are important for librarians to understand especially when discussing potential uses of the mashup with programmers or other technology-oriented professionals. An attempt will be made to reduce these concepts to nontechnical terms wherever possible.

WHAT IS A MASHUP?

Simply defined, a web mashup is a hybrid application whose content and functionality result from combining together third-party data sources. The resulting interactive web application is often an entirely new and innovative service. Mashup is a colloquial phrase from the pop music scene, where it refers to a new song that is mixed from the vocal and instrumental tracks of two different songs. The mashup is often used synonymously with the concept of Web 2.0 and can be viewed as a situational application that can be developed to meet very specific needs of a very specific customer group. The web mashup represents a new class of software applications and is breaking the traditional design approach of standalone systems. Unlike standalone systems, mashup applications can be prototyped very quickly, require significantly less development effort, and are much more dynamic in their development and evolution.

As with many new Internet-based technologies, initial mashup applications have tended to be more of a novelty than practical. It was not until the release of the Google Maps application programming interface (API) that the popularity of the mashup took off. One early notable use of the technology is ChicagoCrime, an application that mixes police data from the Chicago Police Department's database of reported crimes with the interactivity of Google Maps. The result was a mapping site that provides a graphical representation of where crimes were being committed. Almost 600 Google Maps mashups are cataloged in the Mashup Feed database that overlay maps with anything from gas prices, to hurricane tracking, to cell phone coverage, to locations where scenes from a particular movie were filmed.

The emergence of photo hosting and social networking sites like Flickr has also led to a variety of interesting applications. Since many photo sites encourage the input of metadata, designers can mash photos with other information that can be associated with the metadata. One such result is what has become known as Geotagging. Geotagging involves creating latitude and longitude tags for Flickr photos that detail exactly where the photo was taken. In Flickr Maps, photos taken at a specific location are represented by a dot containing the number of photos that were collectively taken and then geotagged by all Flickr users. Such geotagged photos could be used in many ways. For example, an individual researching the residential homes designed by Frank Lloyd Wright could not only view photos of the homes, but could also identify where each is located geographically. Photos with similar geotagging could then be stitched together to create a virtual tour of any one of the homes.

The potential combinations of data sources that can be used in creating a mashup are virtually as limitless as the number of information resources available on the web.

SERVICE-ORIENTED ARCHITECTURE AND WEB SERVICES

Before continuing this discussion of mashups, the concepts of *service-oriented architecture* and *web services* need to be introduced.

Henry Ford's original automobile assembly line process was revolutionary. Time would reveal, however, that the process had serious technology design flaws. The most significant of these flaws was that all of the machine tools used to produce and assemble parts were created specifically and fixed in place for the Model T. Ford did not change the basic design of the Model T for almost two decades, due to the significant costs of retooling the assembly line. Traditional computer software development is based on a similar architecture, where everything required including data, the core application, and the interface are fixed within the program. The online catalog is a great example of this design approach. The bibliographic data, the application that searches that data, and the user interface are all fixed within the online catalog system. Much like the Model T, the amount of resources required by library system vendors to retool are significant. The result is that there is often many years between new versions. The costs associated with retooling also help to explain why libraries rarely switch from one online catalog system to another.

Ford's assembly line shortcoming was partially resolved by General Motors. GM used a flexible manufacturing approach in which subassemblies were created at different factories where interchangeable tools were used. This allowed GM to make changes to any of the subassemblies without disrupting the manufacturing process. Until the 1980s, American car manufacturers would design a new chassis, new transmission, or new suspension parts for each model. During an annual "changeover," the manufacturing plants would retool for the next model year. In service-oriented architecture (SOA), the software design approach separates the data, application, and interface. This allows each level of the application to be implemented with the best technologies for the tasks.

Much like GM's approach to assembly line manufacturing, with the SOA system architecture model the individual software pieces are build independently and can either be interchanged or repurposed. If a library were to build an online catalog using the SOA model the bibliographic data, the core application, and the user interface would be designed as individual software modules. This modular approach to system and service development facilitates the flexibility and responsiveness required in a changing environment. This approach also simplifies complex processes and technologies, resulting in low-cost, reusable components and the ability to create services beyond what they could create themselves.

Using the web as an application platform can boost creativity and shorten development time by removing redundancy in the coding process. Developers can create applications that are built on top of other applications. Using the SOA model, libraries can also build information systems with reusable components, or services that can potentially reduce the long-term management costs. Such systems would enable libraries to more easily share common data between various systems. An interface subassembly could be redesigned and replaced without disrupting the application and bibliographic data processing subassemblies. SOA can enable libraries to create more dynamic library systems that can evolve and adapt to the changing environment much faster than traditional designs.

The concept of *web service* is directly tied to SOA. In this context, web services allow applications to communicate more easily using web-based protocols. Another way to think about web services is that they are websites that are designed for other computers to use. It is important that the concept of web services should not be confused with services available on the web. For example, WorldCat is a service provided by Online Computer Library Center (OCLC) using the web. A WorldCat web service would allow developers to access the raw bibliographic data in the creation of new systems. Unlike library-specific protocols that never gained adoption by other industries, such as Z39.50, web services are not library-specific. The adoption of web services can help lead libraries away from standards particular to the library world and facilitate system interactivity with content publishers and commercial information providers.

Amazon.com was one of the first companies to use web services to open up its technology for other organizations to use. Through its web services, Amazon.com exposes its content and e-commerce tools to software developers and website owners, allowing them to leverage the data and functionality that Amazon.com uses for their own services. Among the functionality that other organizations can use is product information, images, pricing, and the search function. eBay is another example of an application using web services. The auction site's developer section provides in-depth information about deploying more than 100 web services that allow developers to communicate directly with the eBay database and build custom interfaces and applications that can connect to those services.

Together, SOA and web services can allow libraries to deliver services to customers through nonlibrary interfaces and aid in behind-the-scenes search and retrieval services. For example, a library customer could access a library website to request a document. The online interlibrary loan management system could use a web service to communicate with OCLC or commercial suppliers to identify other libraries that could fulfill the request. Assuming all the potential suppliers also make use of web services, the request system could then communicate directly with any of the suppliers to locate the item needed. During this process the customer receives messages updating them as to the progress of the order. The resulting service is a seamless system of communicating and exchanging information using nonproprietary, nonlibrary specific standards.

The adoption of the SOA and web services information infrastructure in the form of mashups allows libraries to use and improve information resources contributed by others while customizing its delivery to local customers. For example, consortia libraries could work together to build systems sharing common bibliographic data and then build customer interfaces and search systems that look and work quite differently. The adoption of SOA and web services models can enable libraries to evolve into stronger organizations at the very moment in time that the use of libraries is becoming just another piece of the customer's information-seeking experience.

DEVELOPMENT TOOLS AND PROTOCOLS

As mentioned in the introduction it is difficult to discuss mashups without introducing technical terms and acronyms. Before the discussion can go on a basic introduction and description of the tools and protocols used in mashups such as API, XML, SOAP, and REST is needed. It is also important to note that REST and SOAP represent two different design philosophies that have been a point of debate among developers, not unlike that of Mac OS versus Windows. A detailed explanation of the two is beyond the goal of this chapter, which is to introduce the concepts.

API

API stands for Application Programming Interface, which is an interface to an application's functions that does not require access to the underlying computer code or a detailed understanding of the application's internal workings. APIs are made available by websites to make their content and functionality more easily accessible. Developers often protect their APIs at all costs since they can be the most important part of a program. Some companies, like Microsoft, deliberately make its API information public so that third party developers will create software utilizing their data, functionality, or platform. The availability of APIs has been the single most important development that has led to the evolution of the mashup.

XML

XML stands for Extensible Markup Language and was defined by the World Wide Web Consortium in 1996. XML is a markup language much like HTML but with fundamental differences. While HTML was designed to display data and focuses on how data looks, XML describes data and focuses on what data is. XML is essentially a method of placing structured data into a text file. XML does not replace HTML but is similar in that both make use of "tags." HTML defines what each tag and its attributes mean, but XML uses tags to delimit data chunks and leaves interpretation to the application reading it.

AJAX

Ajax refers to *Asynchronous JavaScript and XML*. AJAX is not a mashup-specific technology, but is often used in their creation. This technique allows for the asynchronous loading and presentation of web content. When used together, these technologies exchange small amounts of data contained on a web page rather than reload and rerender the entire page. For example, the portion of an online retailer's web shopping cart that contains the items to be purchased could be updated without having to refresh the entire page. Since only a part of the web page requires updating web page rendering and refreshing is much faster.

.NET

This is an umbrella term for an integrated development environment that is at the core of Microsoft's web services strategy. There is a lot of connection between XML and .NET. XML is the glue that holds .NET together. The .NET framework (pronounced "dot" NET) takes advantage of technologies built into the Windows operating system to provide more predictable program security and behavior. .NET is platform independent so a program written to use the framework should run without any changes on any type of computer for which the technology has been implemented. .NET applications can be developed to interact with the Internet from a wide range of devices, including smart phones and personal digital assistants (PDAs). In this context, .NET has been compared to the Java programming language.

REST

Representational State Transfer (REST) is an architectural style for building networked applications. The most common analogy for what REST does is cut and paste. The resource is defined by cursor positions and highlighted selections. Once cut or copied the data is retained in a number of forms so that, when pasted, the richest format understood by both applications is used. Blog sites are mostly designed using REST since they involve downloading XML files (in RSS format) that contain lists of links to other resources.

SOAP

This is one of the fundamental technologies of web services. Originally, it was an acronym for Simple Object Access Protocol, but has been retermed Services-Oriented Access Protocol. To move the data contained in an XML file around different organizations using different software on different platforms it should be packed into a container. That container is a protocol like SOAP. The key components of the SOAP specification are an XML message format for platform-independent communication and a header and a body message structure. SOAP APIs for web services describes which operations or content a service exposes, the format for the messages that it accepts, and how it should be addressed.

RSS

An acronym referred to as either Really Simple Syndication or Rich Site Summary. This is an Internet utility that brings content updates from other web pages directly to the desktop. These updates are referred to as "site feeds" and are displayed by a reader known as a news aggregator. While RSS feeds are most commonly associated with blogs, they can also be used by web services in the creation of a mashup.

Screen Scraping

This is the process of using software tools to parse and analyze content originally written and displayed for human consumption, most often using HTML. The lack of an API from content provider forces mashup developers to resort to this technique to retrieve the information they seek to use in a mashup. For example, a mashup mapping library locations can be created by screen scraping a static directory listing of libraries and combining it with the Google Maps API. Screen scraping is often considered an inelegant solution and has inherent drawbacks. If a website changes its look and feel, the developer must change the method of obtaining the content.

WSDL

The Web Services Description Language is an XML-based service that describes the public interface to a web service. It provides a way to describe XML-based web services regardless of communications protocol. It specifies the location of the service and the operations and methods that the web service exposes. WSDL is an integral part of UDDI.

UDDI

This stands for Universal Description, Discovery, and Integration. It is a XML-based distributed directory that enables organizations to list and discover each other, similar to a traditional phone book's yellow pages. The goal of the registry is to streamline online transactions by enabling companies to find one another and make their systems interoperable.

ANATOMY OF A MASHUP

Now that the basic concepts and technologies have been introduced the anatomy of a mashup can be dissected. A mashup application comprises three different components that are separated both logically and physically by network and organizational boundaries. Those components are the API/content provider, the mashup site, and the web browser.

The *API/content providers* are those sites that host the content being mashed. To facilitate data retrieval, API providers expose their content through web protocols such as REST and web services. Most providers require a developer or application ID to access an API. Some services provide one ID to develop many applications while others require an ID for each application created. As already highlighted, the introduction of the Google Maps API essentially began the mashup craze. APIs from Microsoft's Virtual Earth, Yahoo! Maps, and MapQuest spawned additional applications. Consumer marketplaces such as eBay and Amazon.com have released APIs for programmatically accessing their content. Syndication feed mashups can aggregate a user's feeds and present them over the web, creating a personalized newspaper that caters to the reader's particular interests. An example is Diggdot.us, which combines feeds from the techie-oriented news sources Digg.com, Slashdot.org, and del.icio.us.

The *mashup site* is where the mashup is hosted. How the mashup site is constructed is primarily driven by what programming languages are known by the developer. While the design may be influenced by vendor-provided toolkits, most web APIs are programming language independent. Since there is no right way to create a mashup, any variety of programming languages could be used. Mashups can be implemented like traditional web applications driven by server generated content. They can also be constructed using a combination of both server and browser-based functionalities.

The *web browser* is where the application is rendered and where user interaction takes place. Some mashups can be generated directly within the browser through client-side scripting or applets. The benefits of browser mashing include less overhead on behalf of the mashup server and a more seamless user experience. For example, the Google Maps API is intended for access through the browser. Those mashups created using this later approach are the foundation of the interactive Web 2.0 experience.

MASHING UP THE LIBRARY

As of this writing the mashup is just starting to be used as a tool to provide and extend library resources and services. There are a growing number of library-oriented mashups indexed in the *Talis Developer Network's Innovation Directory.*

BioWizard

http://www.biowizard.com
This mashup adds value to PubMed searches. The search results are displayed identical in style to PubMed. However, BioWizard allows for the ability to rank all publications in the database. Users can also post and share comments on any publications in addition to saving or e-mailing any PubMed abstract.

Delicious Library

http://www.delicious-monster.com/
Built on Amazon.com's web services, Delicious Library is a Mac-based media cataloging application that allows users to manage their collections of books, DVDs, CDs, and video games. Materials can be added by either entering them manually or by using a Bluetooth scanner, an iSight camera, or a USB-keyboard-type barcode scanner.

Go-Go-Google-Gadget!

http://www.blyberg.net/2006/08/18/go-go-google-gadget/
This application was the winner of Talis' 2006 "Mashing up the Library" competition. This mashup integrates library information into the personalized home page offered by Google. There are actually four different gadgets that mash up data from a library's catalog. These include identifying currently checked out items, newest materials, hottest materials, and an individual's requested materials. The only limitation is that the library needs to provide the PatREST API, which as of this writing is still being developed (see the REST definition). PatREST is an XML specification developed at the Ann Arbor (MI) District Library as a simple interface to online library services intended to bring library-oriented development tools into the hands of nonlibrarians, the library customers themselves.

Gutenkarte

http://gutenkarte.org/
Gutenkarte downloads public domain texts from Project Gutenberg, and then feeds them to MetaCarta's GeoParser API, which extracts and returns all the geographic locations it can find. Gutenkarte stores these locations in a database, along with citations into the text itself, and offers an interface where the book can be browsed by chapter, by place, or all at once on an interactive map.

LibraryThing

http://www.librarything.com/

LibraryThing is a full-powered cataloging application that searches the Library of Congress, all five national Amazon.com sites, and more than forty-five world libraries. Users can edit their own information, search and sort, and catalog books with their own subjects or by using the Library of Congress and Dewey classifications. Because everyone catalogs together, LibraryThing also connects people with the same books and comes up with suggestions.

Summa

http://www.statsbiblioteket.dk/summa/

Summa is an integrated search system that simultaneously accesses a number of different data sources currently provided to the users of The State and University Library, University of Aarhus, Denmark. Summa searches across all the different data sources and presents results for the user in a single search result sorted by relevance. The Summa website states that "Users don't concern themselves with technicalities such as databases and data sources; first and foremost, they want some relevant resources." The integrated indexing of the different data sources is done in a way that, in most cases, the customer doesn't even experience that the system is doing something fairly complex.

ISSUES AND CHALLENGES

As is the case with many data integration systems, mashups have numerous issues and challenges.

An issue that all developers face is the protection of intellectual property versus fair use. Mashup developers often do not own the data that is being mashed while the owners may not even know that their data is being used. Information providers may find that their content is being used unknowingly through the use of screen scraping techniques. Even a content provider who knowingly exposes content may determine that their content is being used in an unapproved or illegal manner. Some mashups have been redesigned or completely shutdown due to questionable uses of web services data including trademark and copyright infringement. Developers need to make sure that they have followed all the guidelines and restrictions required by the content providers. Conversely, content providers need to decide whether or not they desire to license their content and, if so, they need to communicate the terms of the license.

Since the tools of web development have become commonplace and simple to use, many mashups may be developed by individuals who are unaware or unconcerned about data security. Web services are particularly susceptible to security breaches in that they have a unique set of platform, XML, and messaging processing vulnerabilities. Therefore, some developers may not fully understand the extent to which a web service exposes their applications and are increasingly becoming a target for network attacks.

Data used in a mashup may be made available in a machine-readable format that requires much more human effort in terms of analysis and data cleansing. This requires the developer to request the data from the relevant content providers and then create his or her own machine-readable database. One mashup created in this manner was developed by the journal *Nature*. Their "Avian Flu" site integrates a database of outbreaks gathered from the World Health Organization and the United Nations Food and Agriculture Organization data, which was then mashed with Google Earth.

How a source site manages and maintains its content should be considered before building a mashup based on third-party data. Unexpected changes in API design, mergers and acquisitions between data providers, and simple acts of nature may result in a broken mashup. Additionally, a mashup may also be designed for user input. While this approach enables open contribution, it can also result in incorrect or inconsistent data entry. Either of these two approaches could compromise the value and trustworthiness of the mashup service.

A related challenge that developers face is determining if the data being used is real. Without an exchange of encrypted ID certificates between the data source and mashup, the data could be coming from a "spoof" site. For example, a hacker could easily feed false data into the ChicagoCrime location mashup, perhaps as an effort to help raise property prices in a particular area by making it appear crime-free. Reputable content providers should employ authentication and authorization schemes for information that involves licensed subscriptions or sensitive data.

FINAL THOUGHTS

It is still unclear to many in the library community that the *mashup* represents a significant new model for resource creation and management. The adoption of SOA design approach to system design could reduce long-term costs by providing shared or third-party applications and services. Without the adoption of web services' design principles it will be increasingly difficult for libraries to engage in scalable collaborations within or across institutions.

Before mashups can make the transition from cool toys to sophisticated applications, much work will have to go into distilling robust standards, protocols, models, and toolkits. Like an old-fashioned manual switchboard telephone operator, a mashup developer has to create most data connections by hand. As the number of web services grows, the more difficult it becomes to keep track of all the data lines in order to make the correct connections. Instead of having a lot of operators (developers) with calloused hands, the protocol developers need to begin thinking in terms of automated switches, referred to as a web service "dial tone" With such a protocol in place, library developers would only need to know the number they want to dial. They would listen for the dial tone and "dial" the websites they want to mashup. That's the level of simplicity that is needed.

Libraries have a long history of duplication of effort and a reinvention of electronic services and information systems. The costs of doing so are becoming increasingly high as resources are wasted in repetitive efforts. The network environment that libraries must compete within requires the library community to mobilize the sharing of their collective resources. Libraries need to move common resources to the network level and concentrate on customizing and creating value for their local customers. Libraries need to use SOA, web services, and the mashup to strengthen collaborative efforts if we are to remain significant in the increasingly competitive information marketplace.

SUGGESTED READINGS

Ajax. http://www.ajax.org/ (retrieved November 7, 2006).

"Avian Flu." *Nature web focus.* http://www.nature.com/nature/focus/avianflu/ (retrieved November 7, 2006).

BioWizard. http://www.biowizard.com (retrieved October 31, 2006).

Blyberg, John. "PatREST: Patron RESR v1.1." [weblog entry] *blyberg.net*, August 15, 2006a. http://www.blyberg.net/downloads/patrest_1.1_overview.pdf (retrieved October 31, 2006).

———. "Go-go Google Gadget!" [weblog entry] *blyberg.net*, August 18, 2006. http://www.blyberg.net/2006/08/18/go-go-google-gadget/ (retrieved October 31, 2006).

Breeding, Marshall. "Web services and the Service-Oriented Architecture." *Library Technology Reports* 42, no. 3 (May/June 2006).

ChicagoCrime. http://www.chicagocrime.org/ (accessed October 16, 2006).

Chudnov, Daniel. "More on Dialtone." [weblog entry] *One Big Library*, August 20, 2006. http://onebiglibrary.net/story/more-on-dialtone (retrieved October 16, 2006).

Delicious Library. http://www.delicious-monster.com/ (retrieved October 31, 2006).

Dempsy, Lorcan and Brian Lavive. *DLF Service Framework for Digital Libraries.* May 17, 2005. http://www.diglib.org/architectures/serviceframe/dlfserviceframe1.htm (retrieved October 31, 2006).

Fielding, Roy. "Architectural Styles and the Design of Network-based Software Architectures." Ph.D. diss., University of California, Irvine, 2000. http://www.ics.uci.edu/˜fielding/pubs/dissertation/top.htm (retrieved October 17, 2006).

Flickr Maps. http://www.flickr.com/map/ (retrieved November 12, 2006).

"Geotagging Flickr." http://www.flickr.com/groups/geotagging/ (retrieved November 7, 2006).

Google Maps API. http://www.google.com/apis/maps/signup.html (retrieved November 6, 2006).

Gutenkarte. http://gutenkarte.org/ (retrieved October 16, 2006).

He, Hao. "What is Service-Oriented Architecture." September 30, 2003. http://webservices.xml.com/pub/a/ws/2003/09/30/soa.html (retrieved October 16, 2006).

LibraryThing. http://www.librarything.com/ (retrieved October 31, 2006).

Talis. "Mashing up the Library Competition 2006." http://www.talis.com/tdn/competition (accessed October 25, 2006).

"Mashup & Web2.0API Directory." http://www.webMashup.com/ (accessed October 25, 2006).

Mashup Feed. http://www.mashupfeed.com/ (accessed October 31, 2006).

"Mashups (Web application hybrids)." http://en.wikipedia.org/wiki/Mashup_(web_application_hybrid) (accessed October 16, 2006).

Microsoft Corporation. "Service Orientation and Its Role in Your Connected Systems Strategy." July 2004. http://msdn.microsoft.com/architecture/soa/default.aspx?pull = /library/en-us/dnbda/html/srorientwp.asp (retrieved October 17, 2006).

McLaughlin, Brett. "Mastering Ajax, Part 1: Introduction to Ajax." http://www-128.ibm.com/developerworks/xml/library/wa-ajaxintro1.html (retrieved October 16, 2006).

Murray, Peter. "Defining Service Oriented Architecture by Analogy." http://dltj.org/2006/09/defining-soa-by-analogy (retrieved October 31, 2006).

"OASIS SOA Reference Model TC." http://www.oasisopen.org/committees/tc_home.php?wg_abbrev=soa-rm (retrieved October 16, 2006).

O'Brien, Damien and Brian Fitzgerald. "Mashups, Remixes and Copyright Law." *Internet Law Bulletin* 9, no. 2 (2006):17–19. http://eprints.qut.edu.au/archive/00004239/01/4239.pdf (retrieved October 16, 2006).

The Programmable Web. http://www.programmableweb.com/ (accessed October 31, 2006).

RSS-DEV Working Group. "RDF Site Summary (RSS) 1.0." December 9, 2000. http://purl.org/rss/1.0/spec (accessed November 7, 2006).

Storey, Tom. "The architecture of the web is transforming the way systems are built and services delivered, providing libraries with an opportunity to extend their impact." *NextSpace* 4 (September 2006): 6–11. http://www.oclc.org/nextspace/004/download/nextspace_004.pdf (retrieved November 14, 2006).

Summa. http://www.statsbiblioteket.dk/summa/ (accessed October 31, 2006).

Talis Developer Network. "Innovation Directory." http://www.talis.com/tdn/innovationdir (accessed October 25, 2006).

UDDI.org. http://www.uddi.org/ (accessed November 15, 2006).

W3C. "Extensible Markup Language (XML)." September 11, 2006. http://www.w3.org/XML/ (retrieved November 7, 2006).

W3C. "SOAP Messaging Framework." June 24, 2003. http://www.w3.org/TR/soap12-part1/ (retrieved November 7, 2006).

W3C. "Web Services Description Language (WSDL) 1.1." March 15, 2001. http://www.w3.org/TR/wsdl (retrieved November 15, 2006).

W3C Working Group. "Web services Architecture." February 11, 2004. http://www.w3.org/TR/ws-arch/ (retrieved Oct 25, 2006).

7

ONLINE SOCIAL NETWORKING
Brian S. Mathews

Online social networking has become a communications phenomenon. Social websites have become extremely popular among teenagers and young adults; however, the appeal extends to a wide range of users. This chapter will serve as an introduction to online social networking, describing the core set of features and highlighting several of the leading websites. Additionally, this chapter will examine criticism, explore opportunities, and provide recommendations to libraries.

WHAT ARE SOCIAL NETWORKS?

Social networking isn't new. The old saying "it's not what you know, but who you know" still rings true today. While online versions of social networks have magnified this concept, the foundation remains the same. Essentially, social networks represent the collective body of the people we know. The primary level is composed of family, friends, and coworkers: typically individuals known in person. Upon extending this initial network, a secondary group of contacts emerges. This level represents the friends of friends. As more layers are added, the reach of social linking continues to expand.

The term social networking was coined by J. A. Barnes in 1954 and has since been studied by a wide range of disciplines, including anthropology, psychology, organizational studies, and information science. At the heart of social networking theory is the idea that relationships are nodes on a map (see Figure 7.1), which can be connected and analyzed. The value and strength of these degrees of association can be measured by their level of integration. Essentially, a strong network is characterized by commonly shared ties or acquaintanceship between individuals, whereas a weaker network is one with limited interconnectedness amongst the group.

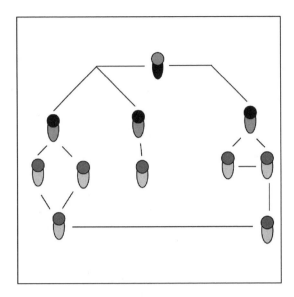

Figure 7.1 Example of a Social Networking Relationship Map.

This interpersonal networking concept originated in 1929 by Karinthy Frigyes, who speculated that we are all connected to each other. The theory is based on the notion that acquaintances grow exponentially as more links are added to the chain. This model evolved into the "small world phenomenon" asserting that everyone in the world can be reached through a short chain of fewer than six acquaintances. This hypothesis was developed and tested in 1967 by social psychologist Stanley Milgram, who experimented by tracking the connectedness of sixty participants in Nebraska to an individual in Massachusetts. A modern demonstration of this theory can be found in the popular game *Six Degrees of Kevin Bacon*. The objective is to connect any actor to Kevin Bacon through movie roles using the fewest number of links as possible. Here is an example:

Natalie Portman was in *Beautiful Girls* with Matt Dillon.

Matt Dillon was in *Loverboy* with Kevin Bacon.

The allure of online social networking websites is that not only do they provide a virtual environment allowing members to interact with family and friends, but they also greatly expand the channels to social discovery. While linking directly to acquaintances is one way to use a network, these websites typically offer additional opportunities for finding others with shared interests. This searching ability significantly increases the value of networking websites because of the potential to establish new relationships. Not only do they enable users to see who is connected to whom, but they also allow people to find others based upon keyword descriptions.

CORE FEATURES

There are many types of social networking websites and they all strive to reach a target audience. While some seek wide mainstream appeal, others focus on attracting niche groups. However, despite the differences, most of these websites are built around a core set of features.

User Profiles

The user profile is how individuals describe themselves to others. Common profile fields include age, geographic location, relationship status, education and employment history, as well as hobbies and interests. Each website varies in the degree of details provided, and most allow for members to leave select fields empty if they do not wish to post the information. The interests section of the profile is where members can personalize their identity. This section typically encourages members to list their favorite music, movies, television shows, hobbies, as well as other entertainment and recreation activities.

Friending

Friending is the process of connecting an individual profile to another member. This action builds the network by linking users together and usually requires two-way authentication with one member initiating a request and the other member approving. In this regard, each person endorses the relationship and enters into a common social circle. Friending also allows other members to see the interconnectedness between individuals.

Groups

Groups are virtual environments for members to gather based on a shared interest. While an individual may list a hobby or an affiliation on his or her profile, by joining a group he or she can interact with other members. Groups tend to focus on a topic, such as politics, religion, sports, video games, or fan clubs. Most provide a threaded message board, file sharing, and other features enabling group members to communicate. Groups that members join are also commonly noted on individuals' profiles, allowing others to see their interests.

Individual Messaging

Social websites usually include a basic messaging system for internal communication between members, which does not work with outside e-mail accounts. Messages are often limited in length and do not include attachment functions. Some websites also limit the quantity of messages individuals may send over a period of time as a method to control spam or other misuse.

Announcements

Announcements are designed for members to send short messages across their network of friends. These statements are usually separated from the individual messaging system and are intended to quickly express news, emotions, updates, or to pose a question to their community.

Individual Message Boards

Message boards are often provided on each individual's profile and available for friends to post comments or ask questions. These boards provide a quick method for members to communicate with each other in a public forum, which is open for all others to read. Commonly posted comments include invitations or recaps of social activities, as well as sentimental expressions. Members often post responses on each other's boards, dialoguing across multiple profiles.

Photos

These websites allow members to upload photos into a gallery that is linked to their profile and open for others to see. The number of images, as well as size specifications can vary; however, a common feature enables others to post comments associated with each picture. Members can also select an image as their default or main photo to represent themselves on their profile.

Blogs or Journals

Blogs or journal features are built into most profiles. They allow individuals to post reflections, news, and updates and often have varying degrees of privacy, ranging from publicly viewable to friends-only. Some websites also allow for personalized features such as current mood, a music play list, and other social indicators.

Icebreakers

Some of these websites provide symbolic displays to express interest in other users. For example in Facebook, one member can "poke" another as a means of gaining attention. This can be done through a wide range of devices, and is kept private between both members. The feature provides the opportunity for a member to initiate interaction and, if the other party is interested, the chance to respond and begin a conversation.

Searching

Searching is powerful feature on social networking websites, since it enables members to locate others based upon set criteria. User profiles serve as description tools, which can be searched, and lead to social discovery or new relationships and consequently, the expanding of an individual's social network.

Privacy Controls

Privacy controls vary, but they typically give members the capability to block specific users, as well as to close off portions of their profile to anyone who is not a part of the accepted network.

NOTABLE SOCIAL NETWORKING WEBSITES

The following summary illustrates the wide range and scope of social networking websites.

MySpace

MySpace, the largest social networking website with well over 100 million members, is one of the top ten most-visited domains on the web. It offers a wide assortment of features including blogs, groups, photo galleries, and message boards. Users have the ability to customize pages using HTML/XHTML and CSS, and to embed music and video into their profiles. MySpace has attained mainstream success by attracting both amateur and professional artists and entertainers, including musicians, filmmakers, authors, and comedians; and it continuously strives to be a cultural supplier and digital media destination.

Facebook

Facebook started out as a social networking utility at Harvard University and has since expanded to include high schools, colleges, corporations, nonprofit organizations, and geographic networks. Despite this vast distribution, Facebook is commonly associated with higher education, and an estimated 85 percent of college students have accounts. Facebook features unlimited photo uploads, groups, blogs, message boards, and a powerful full-profile searching capability that includes subject discipline, dorm, and course enrollment. A unique aspect of Facebook is that individuals may only view the profiles of their friends and of other members belonging to a prescribed network defined by registered institution or a geographic region.

LinkedIn

LinkedIn is a business-oriented social networking directory with over 8 million registered users and reaching across 100 industries. This website allows members to find and post jobs, search for people and business opportunities, and build a network of professional contacts. LinkedIn uses a "gated-access approach" that limits direct contact with other members who are not within an expanded network of friends.

LiveJournal

The blogging website LiveJournal hosts millions of personal journals. Users can create profiles that include interests, geographical location, educational affiliations, and photos. Unlike the other social networking websites, LiveJournal emphasizes the blogging utility. The strength of the LiveJournal system is the ability to "friend" other members, connecting journals to form a common community.

SOCIAL COMMUNITIES 2.0

Online social networking is designed to encourage individual expression, self-discovery, and social interaction. These websites illustrate the dynamic shift away from the static web and leap toward the next generation of user-created content. A large appeal of these websites is that they bring a wide collection of features together in one destination. This diversification makes the online experience more efficient, since users will not have to visit multiple websites. Online social networks are also constantly upgrading, expanding, and adding new features based upon feedback. For many users, these websites are much more than mere social tools, but rather represent an online experience centered on their personalized community. The user is the focal emphasis and members can develop a sentimental connection with others through their interactions online. While these websites bridge the gap for users separated by distance, they can also enhance and complement offline relationships. These tools constitute a defining experience and a ubiquitous communication channel for many users who view these sites as an extension of their social lives.

THE DARK SIDE OF THE SOCIAL WEB

As social networking websites continue to gain popularity, new threats and dangers are emerging.

Online Predators

The threat of online predators has received a lot of media attention, resulting in a Congressional investigation of the crisis. Since these websites promote an open web environment of unregulated content, the protection of members is difficult to provide. Individuals may use these websites to distort themselves, assuming a false identity and assimilating into a community that tends to be trusting. Although privacy controls are becoming more sophisticated, assurance of authenticity will continue to be a problem. Promoting awareness of online deception is an important step toward combating this danger.

Spyware and Viruses

Concern is growing about the spread of malicious software through social networking websites. Teenagers tend to be less cautious of the information they encounter online, believing that social networks are a safe environment. An emerging approach is to exploit these vulnerabilities through embedded links within profiles, often leading to viruses or spyware. These profiles are deceivingly designed to resemble real people. Users will mistakenly accept them into their network, unaware of the vulnerabilities.

Identity Theft and Stalking

Social websites reveal a large amount of personal information and there is concern about the potential of identity theft. False impersonation can lead to financial fraud, as well as damage to an individual's reputation. In several cases, identities, including photos and personal information, have been replicated and used for initiating social relationships with other members. Stalking is another potential risk. Users tend naively to disclose private and intimate details of their lives, assuming that the audience consists exclusively of friends. The social web encourages open interaction; however, unwanted and obsessive attention may result in extreme cases.

Cyber-bullying

The emergence of cyber-bullying is another concern, since users can hide behind anonymity. There have been examples of individuals using the web to harass, annoy, or threaten others. Social networking websites can amplify this problem since users can create false profiles and leave slanderous comments designed to embarrass or defame other members. Social networking communities can also foster the spread of rumors and false information. Since these actions occur online, members may develop a false sense of security and empowerment, distancing themselves from any real-world consequences. Victims usually have no means of recourse since these environments are typically not moderated.

Invasion of Privacy

Many public instances demonstrate the damage that the social web can have on an individual's reputation. Profiles may reveal much about conduct and personality, and the posting of derogatory comments as well as questionable or incriminating photos can have long-term ramifications. Potential employers may be discouraged by what they find out about an applicant online, and current employers could monitor the personal lives of staff. Police and school administrators have also reportedly used social websites to track underage drinking, drug use, and other dubious behavior. This issue of privacy is critical, since users are often unaware that their actions online have possible consequences.

Addiction

The growth in popularity of social networking websites has given rise to the concern that users are replacing real-life experiences with a virtual substitute, which could hinder long-term social development skills. Another implication is that online friendships are often characterized as superficial, with the emphasis being placed on the quantity of acquaintances, rather than on the quality or authenticity of the relationship.

AN OPPORTUNITY FOR LIBRARIES

Social networking websites provide new and exciting opportunities for libraries to interact with patrons. The emergence of the Internet has made information more accessible and is consequently reshaping the future of libraries. The growing public preference for and reliance on search tools, such as Google, is forcing libraries to reexamine their roles and identities, and to rethink strategies toward remaining visible and valuable to users. The rise of the digital lifestyle is also influencing patron perceptions and behaviors. The focus is shifting away from the traditional library as place and to-ward a more ubiquitous presence, striving to meet users where they are. It is vital that libraries remain aware of these societal trends and attempt to accommodate patrons however possible. The following suggestions highlight the potential that online social networking provides to libraries.

Speak Their Language

Appealing to younger patrons is a challenge that many libraries face. With the de-mand for instant gratification and the assumptions of immediate access to information online, the role and purpose of libraries can appear somewhat unclear. Many libraries have responded by increasing entertainment holdings to include movies, music, and video games. Social networking websites enable libraries to enter the social sphere of these younger patrons and to present a modern image. Just as the web has evolved from static to dynamic, libraries should grow too.

The social web can help libraries gain the attention of patrons by increasing acces-sibility and transparency of services. Listing and linking to popular movies, musicians, and other media celebrities demonstrates an awareness of patron interests and provides value, since these items are freely available to them in the collection. An important factor when presenting the library online is not to assume a role of authority or judge, but rather that of a cultural partner. By treating patrons as peers and interacting with them on their turf, librarians can be perceived as genuine allies, leading to a positive impression and potential future usage.

Show Them the Library

A picture is worth a thousand words, and libraries should take advantage of both the photo and video features provided on social networking websites. This is an opportunity to post interesting photos highlighting the character and uniqueness of the library. Patrons may also be encouraged to submit their own photos to be added to the gallery. Other possibilities include uploading floor maps and directories, renovation plans, snapshots of local politicians or celebrities in the library, upcoming speakers or presenters, and photos from past events.

Video content represents another opportunity that libraries can pursue. Many aca-demic libraries bury instructional tutorials on their websites; by also placing them within these social communities, they could increase exposure and use. Libraries may also create brief promotional videos emphasizing the collection, games and activities, and various aspects of the building. Library tours and orientations, as well as clips from workshops, special presentations, and other events could serve as publicity tools. It is important to actually show the library to patrons, who might be unfamiliar with the wide range of offered services, events, and resources.

Assessment

Many libraries use various assessment tools, such as surveys and focus groups, as an attempt to better understand how patrons perceive facilities, as well as to determine future directions. One limitation of this approach is that it preestablishes the concept of what libraries should be, restricting the imagination by not considering what libraries could become. Social networking websites enable librarians to gain unfiltered and unbiased opinions of patrons. By reading publicly posted blogs, librarians can understand the needs and frustrations of users, as well as seek opportunities to provide assistance or clarification. This insight can also allow librarians to see how patrons actually use facilities and resources, which may be different than responses captured through formal assessments.

Repackage Information

The information-seeking process has changed so dramatically that many younger patrons are unfamiliar with traditional research practices. However, librarians using social networking websites can deliver information tools via this social context. By using blogs and message boards to promote resources or answer questions, librarians can interact with patrons using a framework that is familiar to users. The Hennepin County Public Library has taken a progressive step by embedding a catalog search box into their MySpace profile, enhancing access to their collection and furthering exposure among new users. It is important that libraries consider alternative methods and environments that patrons are already using, and seek ways to repackage content in order to fit this evolving world of the social web.

Event Promotions

Social networking websites can be efficient for promoting classes, workshops, and other events. Many of these websites offer interactive calendar features ideal for listing activities. Other tools, including invites, blog postings, announcements, and message boards, allow for wide distribution of library promotions. Direct marketing is another option, since these networks support sophisticated search tools that can be used to target niche audiences.

Outreach

Telephone, e-mail, and virtual reference are valuable services that extend the support of the library beyond the physical walls. These methods, however, require that the patron initiate formal contact. Social networking websites allow librarians to adopt a new role by placing themselves into a social realm with users. By reading blogs, group postings, and message boards, the librarian becomes an active participant, who is able to anticipate and advise patrons as needs arise. Linking to patron profiles also keeps the library within the consciousness of users, potentially increasing interaction. Ultimately, social networking can reduce barriers and encourage a more personal connection between libraries and their users.

Educating Patrons

Social networking websites provide an excellent opportunity to educate patrons about the dangers associated with the web. Rather than blocking access to these websites, librarians should embrace an advocacy role and provide information about online safety. Librarians can also educate parents about the social web, discussing both the value and concerns, and seek to clarify any misunderstandings perpetuated by the media. In this capacity, libraries can provide an important service and gain positive exposure within their communities.

Libraries could also sponsor introductory classes on web design basics since many of these websites enable users to customize their profiles. By offering a series of workshops on subjects such as HTML, CSS, video and photo editing, as well as Flash and graphical design, libraries may entice younger patrons with content they value.

Word of Mouth

Ultimately, online social networks can personalize the library experience for current users and potentially attract new ones. Social web tools allow libraries to demonstrate value and to provide positive and relevant encounters. The greatest publicity is not generated from within, but rather is delivered in the form of peer endorsement. By reaching out to patrons online, others will observe these interactions and become more aware of library services. The objective is to develop a quality reputation online; satisfied patrons will do the rest.

CRITICISM AND RESPONSE

As the popularity of online social networks continues to rise, some debate exists about the role that libraries should play.

- *These websites are for personal and social use, librarians don't belong there.*

While it's true that these websites are used primarily as social channels, the focus is toward building a community of members. Social networks encourage sharing, serendipitous discovery, and open communication; libraries belong in the conversation. These websites attract millions of users daily; if a library's mission is to be a cultural and information provider, then it is vital to recognize the behaviors of patrons, and to provide appropriate support when and wherever possible.

- *Are these websites just a fad? Why should we invest time setting up a presence if they will be obsolete in a year?*

Members of these websites enjoy the freedom of expression, instant interaction, and the ability to personalize information. While the popularity of particular websites may diminish over time, the concepts of online social networking are deeply implanted and influencing the direction of the web. Social web tools are influential and libraries should embrace this participatory opportunity. It is important to avoid settling into one particular networking environment, but rather, to monitor trends and continue to push the library's presence into emerging web destinations. Libraries should seek to incorporate themselves into the digital social fabric, as well as permit their systems to evolve into a more user-driven experience. Much can be gained by exploring these websites and, consequently, user expectations will continue to become more sophisticated. Libraries need to be prepared and able to respond in order to stay relevant. More than anything else, online social networking enables libraries to develop a new and interactive relationship with users, and staff should explore the advantage for as long as possible.

- *Will teenagers want to interact with librarians?*

Social networks can help librarians reinvent their image for a new generation. By bringing services and resources into the accustomed domain of younger patrons, librarians can establish a genuine connection and gain credibility. However, librarians should not assume a role of authority, control, or judge, but rather one as an equal participant. Librarians should use this forum as an outreach opportunity and not simply as a promotional tool. By reshaping the user's experience and increasing accessibility, user perceptions will change, and patrons will choose to interact based upon that value. While teenagers may not perceive the library as cool, they will respond if it can provide them with personal meaning.

- *All our information is on the library's site.*

The social web encourages self-discovery; content is controlled by the user. While library websites strive to present information in an organized structure, usability may not be intuitive for patrons. The advantage of social networks is that they allow the repackaging of information, and content can be customized for the user. The objective is to provide material in the format that suits individual needs. With a growing user preference for web-delivered content, libraries can't assume their websites are a primary destination to which users turn for help. However, by infiltrating social networks, librarians can reenter the patron's consciousness.

- *Won't this take up too much time?*

The largest investment of time occurs before the launch of the profile. Librarians must understand the framework of the social web and establish expectations, policies, and workflow appropriate to the organizational culture. Many libraries already use promotional channels, such as newsletters, flyers, websites, and e-mail lists, to advertise their services; integrating this information into a social networking structure would require only minimal additional effort. Library staff is accustomed to responding to patrons through e-mail, so adding messages and postings through a library profile would constitute a natural progression requiring only a little extra training. While social networking may add some nominal new tasks, ultimately it is a small investment toward greater exposure of the library.

GETTING STARTED

The following steps can help guide your library's entrance into the social networking environment. Beginners may want to start with MySpace since it has many core features, the largest audience, and a relatively simple user interface.

Step 1: Explore

Before building a presence for your library, create a personal account and explore the capabilities of the website. It is important to understand the culture of the social web, and not simply try to replicate your library's homepage. Spend this initial period reading blogs and message board postings and exploring the music, video, and podcast utilities, as well as the search, chat, and photo gallery tools. Treat your experiments as a chance to observe users in their native environment and understand how they communicate. Joining several groups and interacting with members based upon a shared topic of interest may also prove beneficial. Once you gain a sense of how the networking community functions, then you will be ready to contribute to it.

Step 2: Set the Ground Rules

The first decision to make will be who maintains the library's presence: will it be administered by one person or by a team? Social networking websites do not require extensive knowledge of HTML or any advanced programming skills, and hence can accommodate a range of experience levels. Since an effective profile is one that engages users and is updated regularly, seeking contributions library-wide and inviting staff involvement is advisable.

Workflow is the next component: when and what content will be added; who will post it; and who will respond to messages, approve friends, and advertise to users? Staff should have a mutual understanding of these expectations and a shared vision of the image the library will portray, as well as an agreed-upon level of service and interaction that the library intends to provide. Although some organizational cultures may require an official policy, the social web encourages freedom of expression and creativity and, therefore, plans should not be too formalized. Once these details are arranged, communicate the goals of the profile to all library staff. An online presence serves as an extension of the library, and shared awareness is advantageous.

Step 3: Add Content

Once the organizational framework is in place, it is time to add content. A general rule of thumb is to not emphasize selling the library—rather, celebrate it. Strive to make the profile engaging and unique. Aim to be a participant in the community, not just a commercial enterprise. Content should be casual, not sterile or authoritative. Social websites are channels not for press release-style communications or details of policy, but rather for fun and creativity. If you are highlighting a new database, don't use the description provided by the vendor or language intended for advanced users. Instead, explain the personal value and "coolness" of the tool and invite discovery.

Photos are another key element, since they will make the first impression. Rather than uploading images that emphasize traditional library characteristics, spotlight distinct features and show how your library is used. Other opportunities for adding content can include loading upcoming events and classes into the calendar, and highlighting your collection using the "interests" section of the profile.

Step 4: Advertise

After setting up your library's profile, you want to make sure it is seen. The value of social networking lies in the interconnectedness of communities. You will want other members to *befriend* you to enable wide exposure; but realize that the quantity of friends alone does not measure success. Rather, you should maintain a focus on the level of engagement and the user's perception of value. By using the browse and search tools, you can identify potential patrons through characteristics such as zip code or school affiliation. Inviting patrons into your networking community is a one-click process; however an exchange of personal messages beforehand is advisable. Members are often inundated with friend requests and you will want to make sure the library stands out. Consideration should also be given toward publicizing your profile through traditional mediums, such as newsletters, flyers, and posters, as well as through digital channels including blogs, podcasts, e-mail lists, and the library website. You could also consider giving a monthly prize or other form of incentive to encourage members to join.

Step 5: Update Regularly

As your community grows, you should to continue to provide new content. Post blog entries regularly and include a mixture of library news, local topics, and other items of community interest to engage members. Use it to promote events and then to upload photos and video content, inviting user comments. The objective of your profile should be to interact with patrons and to make the library theirs; let them see that they have influence in the decision-making process. The social web presents this new opportunity to dialogue with users; to find out what they like or dislike, what they require or would like to see, and how they actually use and perceive the library. This insight can be a valuable assessment tool for library staff to gain a deeper understanding of patron expectations, helping to guide the future direction of services and resources.

Step 6: Have Fun with It!

The value of your social networking experience is ultimately what you make it. These websites provide chance for your library to show personality, present a modernized image, and to encourage conversations with patrons. By taking advantage of the social web, librarians engage users not only in a new environment, but also with a new context. A successful venture into online social networking can bring staff together, spread the message of your organization, and make the library relevant to a new audience. Have fun with it.

SUGGESTED READINGS

Arnold, Thomas. "The MySpace Invaders." *USA Today*, July 31, 2006. http://www. usatoday.com/tech/hotsites/2006-07-31-myspace-invaders_x.htm (accessed November 20, 2006).

Bardon, Debbie. "Online Social Networking for Business." *Online* 28 (2004): 25–28.

Barnes, J.A. "Class and Committees in a Norwegian Island Parish." *Human Relations* 7 (1954): 39–58.

Chalfant, Drew. "Facebook Postings, Photos Incriminate Dorm Party-goers." *The Northerner*, November 2, 2005. http://www.thenortherner.com/media/paper527/news/2005/11/02/News/Facebook.Postings.Photos.Incriminate.Dorm.PartyGoers-1042037.shtml (accessed November 20, 2006).

Clemmitt, Marcia. "Cyber Socializing." *CQ Researcher* 16, no. 27 (July 28, 2006): 625–648.

Conway, Steve. *Social Network Mapping & the Analysis of Informal Organisation.* Birmingham, AL: Aston Business School Research Institute, 2000.

Evans, Beth. "Your Space or MySpace?" *Library Journal* 131 (2006): 8–12.

Hempel, Jessi and Paula Lehman. "The MySpace Generation." *Business Week*, December 12, 2005, pp. 86–96.

Hesseldahl, Arik. "Spyware's Growing Arsenal; Purveyors of Malware are Increasingly Harnessing the Popularity of Social Networks and Web Video to Infect PCs." *Business Week Online*, August 16, 2006. http://www.businessweek.com/technology/content/aug2006/tc20060816_466084.htm (accessed November 20, 2006).

James, Kathryn. "Six degrees of information seeking: Stanley Milgram and the Small World of the Library." *Journal of Academic Librarianship* 32 (2006): 527–532.

Karinthy, Frigyes. *Minden másképpen van (Everything is the Other Way)*, Budapest: Atheneum Press, 1929.

Mathews, Brian S. "Do you Facebook?" *College & Research Libraries News* 67 (2006): 306–307.

Milgram, Stanley. Small-World Problem. *Psychology Today* 1 (1967): 61–67.

Morgan, Lauren. "Facebook can hurt employment chances." *The Red and Black*, December 6, 2005. http://www.redandblack.com/vnews/display.v/ART/2005/12/06/439512618c11c (accessed November 20, 2006).

O'Leary, Mick. "Ten Things You Don't Know About MySpace." *Information Today* 23, no. 9 (2006): 53–54.

Reynolds, Patrick. *The Oracle of Bacon at Virginia.* University of Virginia. http://oracleofbacon.org/ (accessed November 20, 2006).

Rheingold, Howard. *The Virtual Community: Homesteading on the Electronic Frontier.* Reading, MA.: Addison-Wesley, 1993.

Scott, John. *Social Network Analysis: A Handbook.* London: Sage Publications, 2000.

Seligmann, Jean and T. Trent Gegax. "The many sides of Bacon." *Newsweek* 128 (September 30, 1996): 62.

Vara, Vauhini. "MySpace, Bye Space? Some Users Renounce Social Sites as Too Big." *Wall Street Journal*, October 26, 2006, p. B1–B5.

Willard, Nancy. "Social Networking, Part 2: A Toolkit for Teachers." *MultiMedia & Internet@Schools* 13 (2006): 18–21.

Williams, Alex. "Do You MySpace?" *New York Times*, August 28, 2006, sec.9, pp. 1–10.

Williams, Pete. "MySpace, Facebook attract online predators." *MSNBC Online*, February 3, 2006. http://www.msnbc.msn.com/id/11165576/ (accessed November 20, 2006).

NOTABLE SOCIAL NETWORKING WEBSITES

Cyworld: www.cyworld.com.
Facebook: www.facebook.com.
Friendster: www.friendster.com.
LinkedIn: www.linkedin.com.
LiveJournal: www.LiveJournal.com.

MySpace: www.myspace.com.
Orkut: www.orkut.com.
Windows Live Spaces: www.spaces.live.com.
Xanga: www.xanga.com.

EXAMPLES OF LIBRARY PROFILES ON MYSPACE

Hennepin County Public Library: www.myspace.com/hennepincountylibrary.
University of Illinois at Urbana-Champaign, Undergraduate Library: www.myspace.com/
 undergradlibrary.
University of Texas, Perry-Castaneda Library: http://www.myspace.com/utlibraries.

8

FOLKSONOMIES AND USER-BASED
TAGGING

Ellyssa Kroski

With Phase Two of the World Wide Web, we usher in a new era of online experience; the age of the amateur. Today's web is no longer the sole province of the tech-savvy. Web 2.0 has embraced the ordinary user with easy-to-use online tools that have enabled everyone to participate. Would-be writers are publishing their works with a click on personal blogs, amateur filmmakers are creating and distributing their videos via massive media-sharing websites, budding radio personalities are hosting talk shows via podcasts, and ordinary people are organizing and cataloging digital objects.

Users have been empowered to affect their own online experience and contribute to that of others. Instead of reading static web pages, users are now cataloging their personal libraries, organizing their favorite bookmarks, classifying digital image collections, and sharing their information with others through new generation social software. And they are doing it by tagging.

The wisdom of crowds, the hive mind, and the collective intelligence are doing what heretofore only expert catalogers, information architects, and website authors have done. They are categorizing and organizing the Internet and determining the user experience—and it's working. No longer do the experts have the monopoly on this domain; in this new age users have been empowered to determine their own cataloging needs. Metadata is now in the realm of the Everyman.

WHAT IS TAGGING?

Tagging is a new phenomenon, marked by the advent of Web 2.0. The process of tagging involves attaching descriptive keywords to digital objects for the purpose of future retrieval. Tags are a type of metadata, or data about data, which can be applied to web-based resources to facilitate finding them at a later date. With tags, users can label content they create themselves as well as others' digital objects that they wish to mark for future acquisition. Tagging costs the user little in time or effort and is well worth the incentive offered in the creative freedom to categorize their own data. End users employ tagging to organize their digital collections, categorize the content of others, and build bottom-up classification systems.

Blogs

Tagging is a common feature of many of today's social software applications. Blogs are one such application that invites users to tag the content they create. Most blogging software programs allow authors to apply tags to their blog posts as they make them in order to describe or categorize the content within. The practice of tagging blog posts has become so prevalent that 47 percent of all new blog posts created daily (approximately 560,000 out of 1.2 million) have been tagged (Sifry 2006a).

Technorati

http://www.technorati.com.
Technorati is a tool that can be used to search all of those tagged blog posts. It is a real-time search engine that searches the blogosphere as well as other websites, allowing users to perform searches on blog content rather than on web pages alone. Blogs are a medium that updates quite rapidly. Performing a search here, rather than in a standard search engine, will retrieve a results' list with posts created only minutes before. Technorati tracks over 55 million blogs as well as 11 million tags attached to images on Flickr as well as blog posts throughout the blogosphere. Users can set up saved tag searches in the form of Watchlists.

del.icio.us

http://del.icio.us.
Unlike social-networking websites such as MySpace and LinkedIn, which concentrate on developing relationships, social sites such as del.icio.us, 43Things, and Flickr focus their attention on organizing data. On these sites, users tag items for personal retrieval, rather than to assist others in their location, as in blog posts. Users classify their own or other people's data in the public sphere and the social, or community, aspects arise from there as users share and seek out like-minded individuals.

del.icio.us is a social bookmarking website. What that means is that instead of saving a web page link in the "Favorites" (Internet Explorer) or "Bookmarks" (Firefox) folder for future use, the user saves it to their del.icio.us page. The benefit is that it can then be accessed by any online computer since it is no longer stored only locally. As each web page is added to del.icio.us, the user is given the opportunity to add descriptive keywords, or tags, to the link. This organizes data by category or tag. Users can learn what others have linked to and described by a particular tag or just browse others' collections of links.

43Things

http://www.43things.com.

43Things is a giant life goals to-do list. It is a place to add all of those things in life that you have been meaning to do, such as write a book or become a pirate, and see how many other people out there share the same goal. Users can cheer others on in their endeavors or explore what other people in their hometowns are doing. As with del.icio.us, users are offered the chance to add descriptive tags to each goal as they are added to the list. Users can search goals by tag such as "adventure" and "professional" to view what others have listed as corresponding goals.

Flickr

http://www.flickr.com.

Flickr is a digital image storage and management website. It is a place to organize photo collections into albums, tag them with descriptive keywords, and view others' images. Flickr allows navigation by tag or user, as do the previous two sites, as well as by group. Groups are places for users who share similar interests to post their images such as the "Cats in Sinks" or the "Dogs Eating Potato Chips" groups.

TAG CLOUDS

All of the above websites, with the exception of blogs, offer a view of the global "tag cloud." A tag cloud is a textual display of the most popular tags in use within a particular website (see Figure 8.1). The more popular tags appear in larger sizes and a bolder font. In this way, users can tell at a glance what the most dominant tags are within their community at any given time. del.icio.us, 43Things, and Flickr also offer

activism adventure animals architecture art australia autumn baby beach beauty birthday black blue blog blogging book business california camera camp canada career cat celebrity children christmas college computer dance dream europe exercise family flowers friends fun games garden germany halloween happiness health home inspiration italy japan language learning library literature london love marriage meditation money mountains music nature night nyc ocean organization paris party passion people personal photography poetry programming recipes reference research rome romance sanfrancisco school science scotland sex shopping sky snow software spain summer technology texas thailand tokyo travel trees tv university usa vacation vancouver video water web wedding weight white winter work yellow yoga zoo

Figure 8.1 Tag Cloud.

users a personal tag cloud. This presents the user with a view of the tags that are most predominantly in use by them.

In addition to providing a glimpse into the Zeitgeist, or what is currently in the public favor for a particular populace, tag clouds serve as a new form of navigation. Users can click on tags within the clouds to see what they or others have tagged with a specific keyword. In this way they are a discovery tool.

FOLKSONOMIES

As users continue to add tags, a grassroots organizational scheme begins to emerge that has been dubbed a folksonomy by information architect Thomas Vander Wal (2005). A combination of "folks" and "taxonomy," the term has come to mean a nonhierarchical ontology that is created as a natural result of user-added metadata or tagging. In other words, it is an organically created taxonomy that develops as users add tags and they are amassed and combined.

Folksonomies are an excellent example of the "network effect," the notion that a network, or system, improves with the number of users. As individual users tag their items within a website community, their tags are added to the global pool, reflected in the tag cloud, and a folksonomy is born. If there are only a handful of taggers labeling items, the value to be gleaned from their activity is slight. But, as the volume of users adding tags grows, the more robust the folksonomy becomes. It is also worth noting that in the case of the network effect, and also the folksonomy, the value that is added to the whole by the user is actually a side effect of personal use. The motivation for users' involvement in these social sites is to tag items in a meaningful way for future recall, not to create a folksonomy collaboratively. The folksonomy is a byproduct of users tagging their digital objects. The end result is cooperation, but the impetus is personal need.

Folksonomies are an illustration of the collective intelligence at work. A collective intelligence is achieved when a critical mass of participation is reached within a website or networked system, allowing the participants to act as a filter for what is valuable. A folksonomy is created from the aggregate of user-created tags within a website and therefore provides an inclusive categorization scheme reflective of the collective intelligence of that community.

FOLKSONOMY ADVANTAGES

There has been much discussion in the information world about the concept of folksonomy as opposed to the traditional taxonomy with its controlled vocabularies and hierarchical nature. Likewise, there have been many advantages identified with respect to folksonomies and organizing web content.

Inclusiveness

While top-down taxonomies use a controlled vocabulary that is exclusionary by nature, folksonomies include everyone's vocabulary and reflect everyone's needs without cultural, social, or political bias. Because folksonomies include alternative views together with popular ones, they present a unique opportunity to discover "long tail" interests. The long tail, a phrase first discussed by Chris Anderson (2004) of *Wired Magazine*, consists of the interests of the minority that lie at the "tail" end of a power law, or statistical distribution, which charts the most popular topics. When combined, these nonmainstream, or niche interests, far outnumber the popular ones (The Long Tail 2005).

Currency

Tagging-based systems offer a fluidity and currency that is not possible in a controlled, hierarchical taxonomy. Users create tags as quickly as they create content and they are immediately added to the ontology. This flexibility allows swift responses to changes in terminology and to world events. A large taxonomy such as the Library of Congress classification scheme, in which it could take years to add a date of death to an author's authority record, simply cannot compete with this rate of adaptability. In creating traditional classification schemes, the cataloger is put in the position of fortuneteller, in that he or she must predict permanent categories in advance. The problem with this model is that things change; countries change names, computer technology expands, and sometimes groups of people change the way they refer to themselves, i.e., Blacks, Negroes, Afro-Americans, and African-Americans. And in the world of the web, things change fast.

Discovery Potential

Hierarchical taxonomies are designed for finding specific resources whereas folksonomies are predisposed to discovering unknown and unexpected resources. These systems promote exploration and learning as users browse related topics, tags, and users. There is legitimate value in this discovery system as users have the opportunity to locate new resources that they might not ever have come across through searching. Oftentimes users don't know exactly what resources they are looking for at the start of their research. Discovery systems empower users to uncover alternative paths and related resources on their information journey.

Nonbinary Nature

In a traditional classification scheme, a controlled vocabulary must be made in advance in which one category term is selected that includes all related terms. When future objects are cataloged it must be determined that they either fit into a particular category or they do not. In a folksonomy, these items can fit into multiple categories. For example, an image on Flickr could have tags attached such as cat, kitten, feline, tabby, and cute. In a folksonomy the scheme is multifaceted. As Clay Shirky indicates in his discussion of this topic, there is "signal loss" when you merge multiple concepts into just one term. The Library of Congress subject heading for movies is "Motion Pictures." By reducing terms such as movies, film, and cinema to one all-encompassing category, the distinctive meanings of each term gets lost in the translation. While the cataloger might determine that they are similar enough to be considered one-and-the-same for the sake of the scheme, there are those who disagree. As Shirky perceptively identifies, "the movie people don't want to hang out with the cinema people!" (Shirky 2004).

Self-Moderation

Folksonomies are democratic; everyone has the opportunity to add something to the whole. Likewise, these systems are self-moderating. By their nature, they encourage users from an individual perspective to choose tags that appropriately describe items, which will help them to remember them in the future. Similarly, since tagging is done in a public forum, the social dynamic sways users to choose relevant tags, according to Technorati's Dave Sifry (Mieszkowksi 2005). When tagging a new item, many systems offer users a list of the most popular tags used for that resource. The idea is that the most popular terms tend to be the most relevant, just as a frequently cited article or book is considered to hold more authority in the academic realm. Gene Smith (2004) raises the concern that the idea of translating this practice to the web is often met with disdain by librarians.

Follows "Desire Lines"

What we are witnessing with a folksonomy is an expression of the direct information needs and desires of the user. In a traditional classification scheme, catalogers must attempt to read the minds of the users and make determinations based on their estimations of user needs. Since a folksonomy arises as a result of user tagging, it is reflective of the way that they categorize information.

Users create keywords in order to be able to recall their information at a later time and often their tags are reflective of that. According to del.icio.us' Joshua Schachter, "It's basically a way to remember in public" (Mieszkowksi 2005). For taggers, it's not about the right or the wrong way to categorize something and it's not about accuracy or authority, it's about remembering. In this way the categorization is customized for each individual while still serving everyone.

Insight into User Behavior

Folksonomies give us a chance to observe how users tag their own resources as well as what kinds of untraditional categories have surfaced. New categorization types that have emerged include functional tags such as to_read and to_watch. Both of these are temporary tags that are reflective of the adaptive nature of these bottom-up taxonomies. Although they are very subjective descriptors, they are also both useful tags for users who may want to view what others have on their reading lists. Another new categorization trend involves including the self in tags, such as me, mine, my_photo, and my_stuff.

Folksonomies give us an opportunity to observe user behavior and tagging patterns. According to a study of the del.icio.us website conducted by the Information Dynamics Lab at HP Labs, a stable tag pattern emerges after the first one hundred bookmarks are placed for a particular website. They attribute this synchronization to user imitation of popular tags and to a common knowledge base shared by users of the site. As a result, alternative views exist alongside popular ones without being disruptive to the pattern (Golder and Huberman 2005).

Since folksonomies follow desire lines as mentioned above, viewing user language and behavior in this way could help in the future development of top-down taxonomies.

Community

There is a spirit of sharing and community at work in user-based tagging sites. Everyone has a common goal to catalog their own information, but also to share it with others. On sites such as 43Things.com, users cheer each other on to reach common goals, and on Flickr, cat-lovers can join up with dozens of groups dedicated to pictures of the furry felines.

Low Cost

The cost of creating a traditional, hierarchical taxonomy with a controlled vocabulary is quite high. Expert catalogers or information architects are needed to determine the scheme as well as classify individual entities. User-based tagging provides a low-cost alternative for cataloging web resources.

Usability

Top-down classification schemes require a trained or skilled user base. On the web, that isn't realistic, as levels of user expertise and interest vary greatly. Folksonomies have a very small learning curve and are exceedingly comprehensible to the user. In his article on authority, Peter Morville (2005b) discusses the concept of anchoring as an information-seeking behavior. From a psychological standpoint, people tend to be most influenced in decision making by the first piece of information that they come across. Efforts are then made, on a subconscious level, to confirm this found information and avoid opposing viewpoints. So, if users have a predisposition to anchor onto the most findable information out there, an appropriate response would be to provide the user with a system that is accessible or they will find it somewhere else that is.

Web 2.0 is about sharing and connectivity and participation. It is a user-centered era of the web. We are moving away from expert-dictated, exclusionary models of information organization and toward inclusive, participatory ones.

Resistance is Futile

The fact of the matter is that the enormity of information now being published online through new mediums such as blog, wikis, etc. make a traditional taxonomy and controlled vocabulary an impossible solution. The cost and the manpower required would just be too high. Folksonomies, on the other hand, are much more scalable from an economic standpoint. As *Wikipedia* cofounder Jimmy Wales comments, "I wouldn't even want to think of what it would cost to replicate the Wikipedia categories with paid labor" (Shirky 2005b). In the absence of a professionally designed taxonomy, folksonomies are being viewed as a readily available, "better than nothing," stand-in. According to Clay Shirky (2005a), folksonomies are a "forced move," they are coming whether we like it or not. "It doesn't matter whether we 'accept' folksonomies, *because we're not going to be given that choice.*"

FOLKSONOMY DISADVANTAGES

In addition to the benefits to be gained from the collective intelligence intrinsic to folksonomies, there has been considerable debate concerning their flaws. As quickly as such drawbacks are identified, however, supporters of the organic ontologies have provided responses.

No Synonym Control

In user-based tagging systems, there is no controlled vocabulary and therefore one authoritative term does not exist to describe a concept or entity. This is considered a shortcoming when different users describe assets using many different terms to presumably describe the same thing, i.e., cats, kittens, felines, etc. Because of the characteristic lack of control, there is also no way to regulate the use of plurals vs. singular, acronyms, etc.

Supporters respond that the lack of synonym control is a design choice rather than a weakness in these models. As with Shirky's movie and cinema example, the absence of restrictions allows users to choose words that precisely describe their digital assets without the loss of meaning resulting from a controlled vocabulary (Shirky 2005c). Additionally, many social tagging sites provide lists of "related terms" that encourage the use of "popular" synonyms. Nevertheless, this is a major shortcoming of these systems that developers will need to grapple with as they grow in size.

Lack of Precision

As Bruce Sterling of *Wired Magazine* notes, "a Folksonomy is nearly useless for searching out specific, accurate information, but that's beside the point" (2005). As mentioned earlier, folksonomies are discovery systems, without the powerful search capacity of a hierarchical taxonomy. Characteristically, they are going to have low precision rates.

As Lee of Headshift responds, "In practical usage scenarios the trade-off between simplicity and precision makes sense" (2004). Folksonomies are usable and accessible. Although precision is certainly important, it isn't everything. A traditional taxonomy, such as the Library of Congress classification system will allow users to locate relevant resources precisely concerning a topic such as World War II because of the strength of its controlled vocabulary. However, the user must know that the subject heading is "World War 1939–1945" in order to reap the rewards of this system.

Lack of Hierarchy

Folksonomies are flat systems. There are no parent-child relationships, no categories and subcategories. Hierarchy is a distinguishing trait of traditional taxonomies that are able to provide a deeper, more robust classification of entities. Such systems allow users a finer granularity in searching for resources.

According to Joshua Schachter of del.icio.us, adding hierarchy to the folksonomy model would decrease the level of usability and ease of access that are so valued in these systems (Shirky 2005b). As mentioned earlier, in order to maintain the merits of a folksonomy some sacrifices of functionality are made in favor of sustaining a more usable and therefore useful model.

"Basic Level" Problem

Similar to the problem of synonym control is the concern that users will have different ideas about how to tag entities at a basic level as opposed to using a broader or narrower term. Golder and Huberman of HP Labs give the example: "Perl" and "JavaScript" vs. "programming." They raise the concern that "collective tagging, then, has the potential to exacerbate the problems associated with the fuzziness of linguistic and cognitive boundaries" (Golder and Huberman 2005).

As referenced with regard to synonym control, this may be a preference of folksonomies. There is no vocabulary control and as such, users can include all terms that may apply to the entity when tagging without concern for whether it is a basic, more general, or narrower term. Golder and Huberman themselves observe that because of the nature of these systems, people have an opportunity to learn from one another while tagging and categorizing.

Lack of Recall

Recall reflects the ability of a system to return all resources related to a topic. Because of the lack of synonym control, a folksonomy search will not effect a complete results list because of the use of similar tags. A search for "cat" for example will not retrieve resources that have been tagged with kitten, feline, tabby, or even cats. This is a serious limitation of these systems.

Once again I will mention the concept of trade-offs and that although a user may not be able to locate every resource that has been organized in this fashion, the user will find nothing in a system that is too difficult or daunting to use. Flickr CEO Stewart Butterfield points out, "we'll have a million photos of Tokyo, and if the TOKYO tag only gets you 400 of them, it's OK. You're only going to look at 20 of them anyway" (Shirky 2005b).

Susceptibility to "Gaming"

Gaming is similar to spamming and involves an unethical user who propagates links, or in this case, tags in order to corrupt a system. The Blocklevel blog raises a valid point that "malicious users can purposely pollute the 'Tag Sphere' by tagging every bit of content with every possible tag—effectively spamming the system" (Harrington 2005).

This is definitely a possibility with user-based tagging systems. Although popularized by invoking a spirit of cooperation among users, folksonomies are vulnerable as there are always those who don't play nice with others.

THE FUTURE OF TAGGING

Social software applications have begun experimenting with ways to address some of the limitations of folksonomies, such as the lack of hierarchy and synonym control. By grouping similar tags and offering ways to individualize hierarchy, these websites are responding to user needs with regard to the shortcomings of these organizational systems. As tagging evolves, software developers will walk a fine line between refining folksonomic organization and restricting their users' freedom. If tagging becomes too difficult, or the creative capabilities diminish too profoundly, users will no longer have adequate incentive to participate in the activity.

Tag Clusters and Synonym Control

Flickr offers its users a way to refine the results of tag-based searches. When searching this massive image database, users often discover that photos that have been tagged with the same word can have vastly different subject matter. To assist their users with this difficulty, Flickr has devised an added filter for tag searches called clusters. Clusters divide the tagged images into groups of photos containing additional tags with similar meanings. A search for the tag "apple" in Flickr will return clusters with tags that refer to the computer manufacturer, the fruit, New York City, and the OSX operating system. This helps narrow search results to items containing tags that correspond to the user's intended meaning. Sorting images by clusters is not a necessity of tag searches, but an extra exploratory option that is offered to users following their search.

Tag Bundles and Personal Hierarchy

del.icio.us provides a method for users to create an individual hierarchical system with their tags to further classify their bookmarks. Users can assign one-word tags to their favorite web resources in this social bookmarking system, however, this flat level of organization may not always be sufficient. del.icio.us has enabled users to create tag bundles in order to offer added management of their tags. With tag bundles, users can create top level categories, similar to folders, to include existing tags. A user could create a bundle entitled "personal" that could contain the tags: fun, funny, games, travel, and videos. Another bundle could be called "pending" and include tags such as: to_read, to_print, and to_do. Tags may be assigned to multiple bundles concurrently.

Faceted Tagging and Hierarchy

The video log aggregator, Mefeedia has developed a faceted tagging system, offering users some of the advantages of a hierarchical system. Users can browse and navigate tags within the site by several facets including: place, topic, event, people, or language. Tags are assigned to one or more of these facets according to their connotation. In this way, users can click with confidence on the tag "chile" in the "place" category, knowing that they will be directed toward videos about the country rather than the food.

Deep Tagging and Findability

Social media websites such as Veotag, Motionbox, and Jumpcut are offering their users a heightened form of tagging called deep tagging. Users on these sites can not only tag their video and audio files as they upload them, but also have the ability to tag clips and segments within them with descriptors. Other users searching for related content can skip directly to tagged sections of videos and podcasts. This type of tagging presents the opportunity to describe media in a more robust fashion that may aid findability.

LIBRARIES THAT TAG

Already libraries have begun jumping on the tagging bandwagon hoping to provide their patrons with a user-friendly supplement to their existing systems. The Tipton Public Library, St. Joseph County Public Library, Rutland Free Library, and the Newport Public Library to name a few all use Flickr to display images of their libraries. Also taking advantage of the photo management site are 860 members of the "libraries and librarians" group and 313 members of the "librarian trading cards" group.

Libraries such as the San Mateo Public Library and the Seldovia Public Library are tagging recommended web resources with social bookmarking applications such as del.icio.us. Library and librarian groups are tagging scholarly resources on CiteULike, a social bookmarking website for academic citations.

The University of Pennsylvania library has developed their own tagging system called "PennTags," based on the del.icio.us software. PennTags enables users to bookmark and tag books, articles, websites, papers from the web, as well as library cataloging records.

SUMMARY

The advantages of top-down hierarchical taxonomies for library collections are without question. For cataloging the web, however, they just aren't feasible. The Library of Congress, the largest library in the world, holds 130 million items. The blogosphere produces over 1.6 million new blog posts every day, or about 18.6 posts per second (Sifry 2006b). The new, "voice of the people" approach of folksonomies emerges at a time when attitudes about information organization and retrieval are shifting and the technology is developing to support them. The opportunities for learning about user behavior as well as the implications for improving and/or complementing existing taxonomies that these systems can provide are of no small import. We are on the cusp of an exciting new stage of web growth in which the users provide both meaning and a means of finding through tagging.

REFERENCES

Anderson, Chris. "The Long Tail." *Wired*, no. 12.10 (October 2004). http://www.wired.com/wired/archive/12.10/tail.html (viewed October 30, 2005).

Golder, Scott A. and Bernardo A. Huberman. "The Structure of collaborative tagging systems." HP Labs. http://www.hpl.hp.com/research/idl/papers/tags/tags.pdf (viewed November 9, 2005).

Harrington, C. M. "Tag! You're it!" *Blocklevel*, December 9, 2005. http://blocklevel.com/weblog/information_architecture/tag_youre_it/ (viewed October 30, 2005).

Lee. "Can social tagging overcome barriers to content classification?" *Headshift*, August 30, 2004. http://www.headshift.com/archives/002085.cfm (viewed October 30, 2005).

"The Long Tail." *Wikipedia*, November 13, 2005. http://en.wikipedia.org/wiki/Long_Tail (viewed November 13, 2005).

Mieszkowksi, Katharine. "Steal this bookmark!" *Salon*, February 8, 2005. http://www.salon.com/tech/feature/2005/02/08/tagging/index_np.html (viewed November 10, 2005).

Morville, Peter. *Ambient Findability*. O'Reilly Media, Inc., Sebastopol, CA, 2005a.

———. "Authority." Semantic Studios, October 11, 2005b. http://semanticstudios.com/publications/semantics/000057.php (viewed November 6, 2005).

Shirky, Clay. "Folksonomy." *Many-to-Many*, August 25, 2004, Corante. http://www.corante.com/many/archives/2004/08/25/folksonomy.php (viewed November 12, 2005).

———. "Folksonomies are a force move: A response to Liz." *Many-to-Many*, January 22, 2005a, Corante. http://www.corante.com/many/archives/2005/01/22/folksonomies_are_a_forced_move_a_response_to_liz.php (viewed November 22, 2005).

———. "Folksonomy, or how I learned to stop worrying and love the mess." O'Reilly Emerging Technology Conference, March 16, 2005b, San Diego, CA. Transcript by Cory Doctorow. http://craphound.com/etech2005-folksonomy.txt (viewed October 30, 2005).

———. "Ontology is overrated: Categories, links and tags." Clay Shirky's Writings about the Internet, May 2005c. http://shirky.com/writings/ontology_overrated.html (viewed October 30, 2005).

Sifry, Dave. "State of the Blogosphere April 2006Part 2: On Language and Tagging." *Technorati Weblog*, May 1, 2006a.http://technorati.com/weblog/2006/05/100.html (viewed October 30, 2006).

———. "State of the Blogosphere August 2006." *Sifry's Alerts*, August 2006b. http://www.sifry.com/alerts/archives/000436.html (viewed August 2006).

Smith, Gene. "Folksonomy: social classification." *Atomiq*, August 3, 2004. http://atomiq.org/archives/2004/08/folksonomy_social_classification.html (viewed November 11, 2005).

Sterling, Bruce. "Order out of chaos: What's the best way to tag, bag, and sort data? Give it to the unorganized masses." *Wired*, no. 13.04 (April 2005). http://www.wired.com/wired/archive/13.04/ view.html?pg = 4 (viewed November 9, 2005).

Vander Wal, Thomas. "Folksonomy Definition and Wikipedia." Vanderwal.net, November 2, 2005. http://www.vanderwal.net/random/entrysel.php? blog=1750 (viewed November 11, 2005).

SUGGESTED READINGS

"About." Del.icio.us. http://del.icio.us/about/ (viewed October 30, 2005).

"About" Technorati. http://www.technorati.com/about/ (viewed October 30, 2005).

Andrews, Robert. "Public could help BBC to index archive." *Journalism.co.uk*, November 1, 2005. http://www.journalism.co.uk/news/story1583.shtml (viewed November 9, 2005).

Angeles, Michael. "Dan Brown on freetagging." *Urlgreyhot*, April 1, 2005. http://urlgreyhot.com/personal/weblog/dan_brown_on_freetagging (viewed October 30, 2005).

Arrington, Michael. "All the Cool Kids are Deep Tagging." *Techcrunch*, October 1, 2006. http://www.techcrunch.com/2006/10/01/all-the-cool-kids-are-deep-tagging (viewed October 2, 2006).

Bryant, Lee. "Prototypes: BBC shared tags." *Backstage BBC*, May 12, 2005. http://backstage. bbc.co.uk/prototypes/archives/2005/05/bbc_shared_tags.html (viewed November 9, 2005).

Burkeman, Oliver. "G2: Ideas: Folksonomy." *The Guardian*, September 12, 2005, p. 29.

Coates, Tom. "(Weblogs and) The mass amateurisation of (nearly) everything..." *Plasticbag.org*, September 3, 2003. http://www.plasticbag.org/archives/2003/09/ weblogs_and_the_mass_amateurisation_of_nearly_everything.shtml (viewed November 10, 2005).

"Folksonomy." *Wikipedia*, October 26, 2005. http://en.wikipedia.org/wiki/Folksonomy (viewed October 30, 2005).

"Folksonomy? ethnoclassification? libraries? wha?" *Rawbrick*, August 31, 2004. http://www. rawbrick.net/article/844/folksonomy – ethnoclassification-libraries-wha (viewed October 30, 2005).

Lawley, Liz. "Social consequences of social tagging." *Many-to-Many*, January 20, 2005,. Corante. http://www.corante.com/many/archives/2005/01/20/social_ consequences_of_social_tagging.php (viewed November 22, 2005).

Lee. "BBC Backstage prototype: Social tagging." *Headshift*, May 12, 2005. http://www. headshift.com/archives/002498.cfm (viewed November 9, 2005).

Mathes, Adam. "Folksonomies—Cooperative classification and communication through shared metadata." December 2004. http://www.adammathes.com/academic/computer- mediated-communication/folksonomies.html (viewed November 10, 2005).

Maurer, Donna. "Findability vs. discoverability." March 8, 2005. http://www.maadmob.net/ donna/blog/archives/000609.html (viewed October 30, 2005).

Mercado, Andrea. "Tagging on Flickr & del.icio.us." *Library Techntonics*, October 24, 2005. http://www.librarytechtonics.info/archives/2005/10/tagging_on_flic.html (viewed November 3, 2005).

Miller, Paul. "Web 2.0: Building the new library." *Ariadne* 45 (October 2005). http://www. ariadne.ac.uk/issue45/miller/ (viewed November 3, 2005).

Quintarelli, Emanuele. "Folksonomies: power to the people." *ISKO Italia*, June 24, 2005. http://www.iskoi.org/doc/folksonomies.htm (viewed November 10, 2005).

Smith, Gene. "Peter Morville: The tagsonomy interview." *You're It!*, October 19, 2005a. http://tagsonomy.com/index.php/peter-morville- the-tagsonomy-interview (viewed November 15, 2005).

———. "Tagging tags to make synonyms." *Atomiq*, October 31, 2005b. http://atomiq. org/archives/2005/10/tagging_tags_to_make_synonyms.html (viewed November 10, 2005).

Timothy. "Folksonomies in Del.icio.us and Flickr." *Slashdot*, January 4, 2005. http://slashdot. org/article.pl?sid = 05/01/04/0117245 (viewed October 30, 2005).

Todras-Whitehill, Ethan. Folksonomy' carries classifieds beyond SWF and 'For Sale'." *New York Times*, October 5, 2005, sec. G, p. 7.

Udell, Jon. "Collaborative Knowledge Gardening." *InfoWorld*, August 20, 2004. http://weblog.infoworld.com/udell/2004/08/30.html#a1064 (viewed November 20, 2005).

Willms, Jordan. "Gardened hierarchical folksonomy—the next evolution in semantic classifica- tion." *Stream of Consciousness*, June 27, 2005. http://www.jordanwillms.com/index. php/2005/06/27/gardened-hierarchical-folksomy-the-next-evolution- of-web-20/ (viewed November 12, 2005).

Wright, Alex. "Folksonomies redux." September 7, 2004. http://www.agwright.com/blog/ archives/000905.html (viewed November 15, 2005).

9

UP,UP,DOWN,DOWN,LEFT,RIGHT, LEFT,RIGHT,A,B,SELECT,START: LEARNING FROM GAMES AND GAMERS IN LIBRARY 2.0

David Ward

Video games have come a long way since the days of Pong and the first Atari 2600 home systems. With advances in computing technology, graphics, gameplay sophistication, interactivity, and depth of experience, video games have moved from the back rooms of bars and arcades into the mainstream, evolving from a curiosity and toy for youth to a cultural, economic, and social force. Video games clearly demonstrate their new acceptance in the marketplace, with an estimated $18 billion effect on the economy in 2004, and game sales alone generating $8 billion dollars. (Conry-Murray 2006) Generations that now exist have always known games and take for granted the interactivity, sophistication, and responsiveness these systems have come to deliver. The educational community is slowly catching up to the gaming generation and discovering that games can be an effective tool for conveying new kinds of learning and understanding new ways of structuring information-rich instructional environments.

The influence of gaming can be seen in a wide variety of activities, from formal adoptions in the business world to the informal communities gamers form to socialize, share information, and forge identities outside of home and work. The developing gaming presence in libraries is equally diverse, spreading from the design of educational games and simulations to incorporating lessons learned about learning styles and structures from video games into mainstream library activities. Libraries in the near future will need to understand how game design principles, gaming communities, and in-game learning methods can be used to educate the gaming generation about the structure, organization, and critical use of information.

DEFINITION

Kirriemuir and MacFarlane provide a clear definition of video games in their survey of the gaming and education literature that will be used in this chapter whenever "video games" or "gaming" is mentioned. A digital/video game is one that:

- Provides some visual digital information or substance to one or more players
- Takes some input from the players
- Processes the input according to a set of programmed game rules
- Alters the digital information provided to the players

—(Kirriemuir and McFarlane 2006)

This chapter will focus on five main aspects of gaming that impact libraries. Each of these aspects represents an intersection of gaming characteristics and the goals of Library 2.0 posited by Chad and Miller (2005), wherein libraries function as a social milieu that "invites participation" and actively encourages social interactions, using flexible, best-of-breed systems to permeate user experiences in a variety of environment. These five aspects are:

1. Gaming as a cultural phenomenon;
2. Gaming as a place;
3. Gaming as an educational tool;
4. Gaming as a designed interface;
5. And finally, gaming as a tool for collaboration.

Current examples of each characteristic will be given, as well as a thorough discussion of ways libraries can take advantages of opportunities to grow and develop services that take advantage of what researchers have learned about user behaviors and characteristics.

GAMING AS A CULTURAL PHENOMENON

In recent years, gaming has grown to become one of the highest selling entertainment sector industries, with annual sales expected to top $15 billion by 2010 (Conry-Murray 2006). While many traditionally think of video games being played predominately by children or teenage boys, industry surveys show that the average game player is in fact 33 years old, and has been playing games for over 12 years (ESA Facts and Research 2006). Women make up 38 percent of the overall game playing population, while women over 18 (30 percent) represent a larger portion of the game playing population than boys 17 and younger (23 percent) (ESA Facts and Research 2006). Moreover, a 2006 survey showed that women make up 64 percent of the online gaming market segment (Gupta 2006). A 2003 Pew survey of college students found that all of them had played video games at least once, and 65 percent categorized themselves as either regular or occasional game players (Jones 2003). Nintendo recently reached out to older demographics as well, marketing its next generation Wii console to seniors at the 2006 AARP Life@50+ event (Taub 2006).

Considering video games as tangible information objects provides a jumping-off point for libraries looking to join this active and growing community. Video games can be thought of as primary source materials and a new form of literature, with the corresponding activity of gaming as a new form of literacy, wherein the game player actively participates in the creation of the story, making choices along the way that can lead to multiple divergent outcomes. As with other forms of popular fiction, collecting, promoting, and archiving video games serves not just to provide entertainment for today's users, but also to ensure that this material is preserved as part of our collective cultural heritage.

Collection Development

Gaming collections serve a variety of diverse needs and users: entertainment for players, teaching tools and environments for educators, and popular culture artifacts and primary source material for researchers. As a community resource, gaming collections also provide opportunities for programming, a hip and modern tool for outreach and marketing the image of a library, and a safe space within gaming worlds for community activities to take place. Gaming collections today often focus on current games of topical interest to today's generation of gamers, as evidenced in the literature (Scalzo 2005) and through a perusal of gaming collection descriptions at sites like the Library Success Wiki (http://www.libsuccess.org/index.php?title=Gaming#Libraries_Circulating_Games). As gaming continues to become more pervasive and ubiquitous, however, the nature of gaming collections will adapt to include a broader definition of gaming and a wider variety of materials. For example, older (or "vintage") games are in vogue again, thanks in part to software technology known as emulators, which allow PCs to run versions of classic games for older platforms such as the Atari 2600 and Nintendo NES (Lubell 2003). Other games can create unique collecting challenges. The huge popularity of Massive Multiplayer Online Games (see http://en.wikipedia.org/wiki/MMOG) such as World of Warcraft and Everquest makes them likely candidates for most collections; however, the software itself is merely a gateway to the actual networked game service, which is run on remote servers and requires individual monthly subscriptions in order to participate. Games such as these cannot simply be taken home and played "out-of-the-box," but instead require additional hardware, software, and registration requirements that will be difficult if not impossible for libraries to support. Making collections accessible to users (especially for research and teaching faculty at academic institutions) can also require collecting and maintaining gaming hardware, such as the actual consoles themselves, as well as establishing physical areas where collections can be played in-house. In academic and school libraries, collections are evolving to support the curricular use of gaming in such diverse disciplines as art, literature, psychology, speech communications, human factors (aviation), education, history, and specific courses taught in game design.

Archiving

Gaming collections are ripe candidates for the Betamax syndrome, wherein the hardware necessary to access the informational content of games becomes outdated, unsupported, and eventually obsolete. Video games can often have a shorter shelf life in stores than books, and those that aren't top sellers can go "out of print" quite rapidly. And unlike beta or VHS tapes, which can be preserved through digitization or reformatting, video games are not static objects; the game-playing experience and outcomes are often different for every person that plays an individual game, and for future researchers and users to have adequate access to the intellectual content of games, some method must be found to preserve the game-playing experience of a title as well as the actual code and physical object itself.

Current archival efforts include individual collections such as the Stephen M. Cabrinety Collection in the History of Microcomputing at Stanford (http://www-sul.stanford.edu/depts/hasrg/histsci/index.htm), which houses a large variety of video games for a variety of platforms. The Library of Congress is also looking at the bigger picture of preserving games as part of our digital heritage by designating them as a format for preservation for the National Digital Information Infrastructure and Preservation Program (NDIIPP) (Carless 2006). Larger issues in archiving games include resolving copyright concerns from reformatting or using emulator software to play older games on newer PCs, a topic that concerns many game manufacturers who see free emulators as tools of piracy that hamper their ability to repackage and resell older games to a new generation of users (Lubell 2003).

Programming

The social aspects of gaming provide an excellent opportunity for libraries to position themselves within the gaming culture of their communities, using traditional and new types of programming to promote collections and build new types of social spaces. Branston (2006) notes some possible venues for using gaming to reach users, including offering gaming programs where users can actually play or compete in games using library facilities, as well as offering game advisory services as a branch of reader's advisory services. The Ann Arbor District Library (AADL) is well known for its active use of gaming to reach teen users, offering different gaming "seasons" involving tournaments, and creating a blog (http://www.aadl.org/aadlgt) where gamers can keep informed and become involved in the planning and organization of gaming events. As Eli Neiburger of the AADL notes, "[i]f you do not offer them [the gaming generation] something of value now, you will be irrelevant to them for the rest of their lives" (Stephens 2006). Gaming nights have also been successful in academic libraries and provide an opportunity to reach out to college age students and also promote collections to the academic community at large (Sutton and Womack 2006).

Programming for games extends beyond entertainment, however. Gallaway and Lauzon (2006), for example, discuss ways to use games like Dance Dance Revolution (DDR) beyond the typical tournament format. DDR benefits health by increasing heart rate in a manner consistent with other types of exercise, introduces players to a wide variety of world music they may not previously have been familiar with, and helps general visual literacy and physical coordination skills through basic gameplay. Other libraries are using the lure of gaming in classic library tradition to encourage literacy and other activities, by linking completion of tasks like checking out books and writing book reports to access to special gaming privileges, like gaming parties and special prizes (Gutsche 2006). And in academic environments, programming can provide opportunities to inform a university community about the work of local gaming researchers.

Future Programming Possibilities

Some possible future programming activities are already being experimented with, including programming offered in virtual worlds like Second Life (discussed in the next section), as well as the relatively new phenomenon of "Big Gaming." Big Gaming (also called street gaming, urban gaming, public gaming, or pervasive gaming) involves looking at cities as platforms and social games as software that runs on them. An example is the "Come Out and Play" Festival held in New York in the summer of 2006 (http://www.comeoutandplay.org/), where participants dressed up as characters from Pac Man to reenact the game ("Pac Manhattan"), projected a Space Invaders game on a building, played miniature golf on sidewalks, and more. As a public space in cities, libraries are a natural platform for this type of gaming, both in terms of reimagining existing games within library collections, as well as reconceptualizing the library as a space and a content provider that interacts with the city itself.

GAMING AS A PLACE

The development and popularity of MMOG's and virtual worlds such as Second Life has led to a reconceptualization of the social life of gamers, and recent research is starting to cast games as socially important "third places" apart from home and work where social engagement and relationship forming activities take place (Steinkuehler and Williams 2006). Second Life has attracted real world investment from a variety of interests, including car companies like Pontiac (Morissey 2006), concerts from real world performers, large companies like IBM looking for a new way to hold corporate meetings (LaMonica 2006), news agencies such as Reuters that plans to report on real life events in Second Life and Second Life news to real life readers (Terdiman 2006), and a variety of other entertainment and business ventures.

Virtual worlds are becoming real in an economic sense as well, with currency exchanges that trade real dollars for game dollars (Model Economy 2005). Cottage industries are also sprouting up where players of games develop products and services that generate a real world income (Hof 2006). Considering gaming as a new social commons (or a new suburb in which to open a branch library) opens up many exciting possibilities for developing a social and intellectual model for what a library is and how it interacts with its community.

One of the first library uses for virtual spaces has been as a new venue for providing library programming, content, and educational resources. For example, Second Life (http://secondlife.com/), a three dimensional virtual world currently populated by over a million users, allows its participants to purchase virtual land on which they can build anything they like, from recreations of classrooms, to virtual displays and museums, to interfaces for search engines that initiate searches in web browsers. Many businesses, universities, and other organizations are currently experimenting with Second Life as a space for collaborative activities such as corporate training, advertising space, meeting/seminar space, and a space for classes and other educational opportunities from traditional institutions. Harvard, for example, is one of many institutions offering classes taught in whole or in part in Second Life (Foster 2006). Libraries have also set up shop in Second Life—the Alliance Library System, for example, has organized one of the largest and most well known collective ventures on an island in Second Life called "Info Island" (see http://infoisland.org/). Info Island has hosted many programming events, including training for librarians on getting involved in Second Life, book talks, and houses various digital collections (see http://infoisland.org/category/calendar/ for a list of Info Island events). In a sense, Info Island has become a new type of digital branch library for the Alliance Library System.

In addition to simulating traditional real world programming, there are many new activities for libraries to explore that take advantage of the unique characteristics of virtual world design and space. The Role Playing Game (RPG) genre of video games, for example, is in effect a new kind of storytelling medium where users create their own unique stories as they advance through a game. Similar to the "Choose Your Own Adventure" series of books from a generation ago, RPG players become not just passive consumers of story content presented to them by others, but active participants and creators, using their personal gameplay experience as a launching pad for story development. World of Warcraft players already share many types of stories with each other, from descriptions of game playing sessions and quests, to devising elaborate back stories for their characters (see the World of Warcraft forums at http://forums.worldofwarcraft.com/, especially the WoW Role-Playing forums). This suggests a new type of storytelling program, where librarians and users collaborate more as equals to create and share stories about their exploits, using gaming as a tool for content generation and collaboration.

Virtual gaming spaces can also exist as proxies for real world spaces. For example, Starwood Hotels decided to preview their new "aloft" hotel line by hiring two firms to create and then market the model within Second Life (Jana 2006). This allowed them to get feedback on what future customers wanted in the future real world space, without having the expense and logistical problems of creating physical models and then bringing people in to see them. Libraries can do this exact same thing when designing new physical spaces of their own—create a working model in a virtual world space where users can actually walk around and experience the space in 3D, and provide feedback on the best way to physically locate and organize important library features so that the resulting structure is intuitive for most users to navigate.

A final way to look at gaming as a space is from an outreach and marketing perspective, in which the library looks to craft an identity and image within game worlds, and expand the scope and reach of its services to users. In-game advertising is just hitting its stride, with individual video game manufacturers such as EA Sports signing prominent deals to place other companies' ads in some of their games, and the market for in-game ads is expected to hit $400 billion by 2009 (Edwards 2006). Possible avenues for libraries to pursue on this front include advertising libraries and services in relevant games and virtual worlds like Second Life, and also working with game designers and publishers to craft the image and role of libraries and information research skills as they are portrayed in game worlds.

GAMING AS AN EDUCATIONAL TOOL

Increasingly, games are being experimented with in the classroom as both teaching tools and teaching environments, and research into how players learn in games is influencing conventional instruction as well. Much of this research centers around using video games as simulations of real world environments and situations, where students take on identities to solve problems creatively and gain practical experience in the use and application of discipline- and task-specific knowledge. Van Eck notes that "learning that occurs in meaningful and relevant contexts is more effective than learning that occurs outside of those contexts, as is the case with most formal instruction" (2006). Students used to the responsiveness and participatory nature of video games are often not attracted to the dry style of the traditional lecture method, which some see as a "nineteenth century model" of education, characterized by "one tape recorder talking to another" (Foreman 2004). In efforts to capture the kind of learning and involvement that goes on in games, national groups such as the Federation of American Scientists are calling for federal research into how games and models of gaming learning can be converted to educational uses (Not Playing Around 2006).

One of the keys for librarians to be able to utilize the educational potential of games is to first understand how game learning takes place. In his seminal work on video games and learning, James Gee (2003) describes thirty-six learning principles that describe how gamers learn the often extremely complex actions necessary to complete in-game tasks in today's generation of video games. Gee posits gaming as a new kind of literacy, and that in learning to "read" games, the mind is engaged in ways that benefit other literacies as well. Through personally identifying with game characters, players acquire motivation to learn the rules and boundaries of game worlds; actual gameplay then builds skills through a process where users probe and test their world, changing actions in response to failure, and receiving rewards upon successfully learning a winning strategy and completing in-game goals (Gee 2003). MacKenzie (2005) provides an excellent summary of the skills Gee identifies users learn through gameplay, including pattern recognition, system thinking, problem solving, thinking divergently, and strategic thinking. Gaming is also cited for building additional skills for real world professional and business application, including "analytical thinking, team building, multitasking, and problem-solving under duress" (Not Playing Around 2006). The key element, according to Gee, is that "the power of video games, for good or ill, resides in the ways in which they meld learning and identity" (Gee 2003).

In today's classroom, teachers use a combination of repurposed commercial off-the-shelf games (COTS in the terminology of Van Eck) as well as games designed purely for educational purposes (Van Eck 2006). An example of game learning principles in action is found in the work of Kurt Squire, who experimented with Civilization III as a tool for learning ancient history to middle and high school classes. In her study of Squire's work, Shreve (2005) notes that "[g]ames can be an effective way of reaching students who haven't responded to conventional teaching methods, and they can get gifted students to apply critical-thinking, problem-solving, and other higher-level skills to subjects they already know." However she is also quick to point out that "games [should be] used in the classroom only if they truly enhance learning and benefit the students who need it most" (Shreve 2005).

In analyzing the success and interactivity of off-the-shelf games, George Mason researcher Joel Forman notes that "[t]hese virtual settings anticipate advanced online learning worlds that can be dedicated to different subjects, populated by single users and teams, and pedagogically structured for deep and rapid experienced-based learning" (Whelan 2005). Examples of these types of online learning world can already be seen in games like Whyville, a game/virtual world designed primarily for elementary education. As one lesson, Whyville creators introduced a virus called "Whypox" that made characters constantly say "Achoo" when talking, interrupting the flow of the game and consequently disrupting the game's fun. Users then banded together to find out the cause of and cure for the disease, and in doing so learned about real world epidemiology of diseases (Olsen 2006). Other similar next generation games include River City, a science simulation designed by George Mason and Harvard researchers involving a similar detective-like quest to investigate a disease outbreak (Trotter 2004), and the Agricultural Economics Challenge, in which students learn economic principles through running a simulated business (Bocanegra and Harrison-Smith 2005).

There are many options for libraries looking to take advantage of the educational aspects of gaming. Actual library games or virtual worlds along the lines of Whyville and River City can be built, using characteristics and learning techniques from popular genres of games, or alternately elements of library research and information skills can be built collaboratively into these preexisting games to better integrate with an existing curriculum. But using actual games is only one method to incorporate game learning into the library educational mission. Many game characteristics and the game learning principles elucidated by Gee can also be used as conceptual frameworks in the design of library instructional activities. Much as in the world of information searching, players learn by doing (Gee's "Probing Principle") and by discovering (Gee 2003). Gee's "Discovery Principle" states that "overt telling is kept to a well-thought-out minimum, allowing ample opportunity for the learner to experiment and make discoveries," receiving feedback from their environment that must then be correctly interpreted in order to inform their next action (Gee 2003). Through identifying with characters and sharing their goals, players buy into the illusion of the game world and dedicate hours to tasks that they might not otherwise undertake. As part of this process, players are provided opportunities for incremental improvement and smaller rewards along the path to larger ultimate rewards. This incremental improvement leads to development of basic in-game skills that are recycled later in games, with added complexities creating a higher level of difficulty that must be mastered for success in later game tasks.

The work of Gee and others has clear implications for library educational models. Firstly, it echoes other educational research in saying that the lecture as a sole or primary method of delivering educational content is dead. What game learning principles suggest is that libraries move more toward integrated environments that use systematic means of teaching information-seeking skills, by providing users with a situational context and identity to assume that engages them directly with the resources and tools of information research and retrieval. The interactive models resulting from this will cast individual searching skills in the broader context of research as an in-game skill to be learned and the tools and resources for conducting it as the "world" within which users operate and build their knowledge. Actual interactions with librarians then evolve into collaborative discussions in which concepts and skills learned through gameplay are put into real world perspective and related to real world applications.

An excellent example of this model can be found in the educational software "In the Chair," (http://www.inthechair.com/index.php) which was featured at the third annual Web 2.0 summit. This software allows students to play along to sheet music using a computer's microphone to allow the software to listen to and critique student's playing. "The application turns music practice into something closer to a video game," and the role of the teacher then evolves into more of a collaboration to discuss the software's feedback with a student in terms of the larger concepts and goals of music performance and education (Calore 2006).

GAMING AS A DESIGNED INTERFACE

The literature of game and interface design is crucial for designing the world of information access and retrieval, and informs where research tools and interfaces can evolve for the next generation of library searching. Game interfaces are often far more complicated than sites like Google or online catalog interfaces, as Kirriemuir (2006) has graphically shown. Yet, gamers are willing to spend hours learning to master these interfaces, while they often give up in frustration after a few failed searches in library catalogs. Among the key differences between game interfaces and library search tools are the ways in which games are initially designed, and the way in which feedback is provided and digested by players.

Game design principles are closely tied to game learning principles. Specifically, the world that game developers create dictates the methods and kinds of learning that players will need to master in order to become fluent and successful in the game. As Steven Johnson notes in an interview, "[o]ne of the main things that games do is teach us how to play them" (Grand Theft Education 2006). Gamers don't necessarily read directions before they play—the game design allows for them to jump in and start hitting buttons, and learn from the feedback the game provides. Every game presents the player with a designed universe, within which certain rules apply, a certain range of actions can be taken, and a certain range of outcomes is possible. Games can include one or more interfaces through which players experience each individual reality, and from which they interact with their world. Interfaces can be simple and quick to learn, like Pong, with a limited amount of data to be digested and a small number of possible actions, or gigantic, as in games like Grand Theft Auto San Andreas or the Final Fantasy series, which feature multiple interfaces, some with an incredibly dense amount of information and numerous possible actions.

Kirriemuir and McFarlane (2006) emphasize the need to understand what it is that makes games good vehicles for learning, noting that "[r]ather than aiming for an experience that superficially resembles leisure-based 'fun' activities, or one which attempts to conceal the educational purpose, it might be argued that we should understand the deep structure of the games' play experience that contribute to 'flow' and build these into environments designed to support learning." Fortugno and Zimmerman (2005) further describe the game experience as containing elements including "interactivity designed with clarity of input and output; short-term and long-term goals to shape the player's experience, a well-designed ramp for beginners to learn the ropes; and a game structure that actually contains the possibility of genuine *play*, not just quiz-style questions and answers." Game design can also involve gathering and allowing user input and modification as a function of the game—as in the case of the game Quake, where creators specifically made it possible for users to create their own maps and modifications to the game and then share those with other players (Hinton 2006).

Game design doesn't need to be a rigid process that locks out potential modifications and input from users, however, as Hinton (2006) demonstrates by noting that the success of sites like Wikipedia and Craigslist "was that they [the creators] didn't try to micromanage or predict their users' every need and behavior. They merely created the right conditions for achieving what their users needed to get done, and they 'got out of the way.'" Second Life is an example of this type of design; as a game, it doesn't actually provide a set of prescribed goals or quests, as other multiplayer games like World of Warcraft do. Instead, Second Life provides a set of tools for creation and a "sandbox" environment where users are free to do whatever they like. The resulting experience of "playing" Second Life is thus largely determined by the participants themselves, and is scripted as little as possible by the actual game creators.

These game design principles can be incorporated into information architecture design in libraries by thinking of the library itself (and the concepts of information and research embodied by it) as a specifically designed experience and environment, with a set of rules and goals, and actions that lend themselves to discovery through actual play. In developing this model, new types of information architecture would need to (a) identify and account for a variety of short, medium, and long term user/player goals; (b) provide users with tools and a means to create their own tools to achieve goals, and a set of definable actions that govern these tools; and (c) provide rich and varied levels of feedback to indicate success or failure in achieving each goal. As with virtual worlds like Second Life, a well-designed library world should allow for users to create both their own tools for accessing content (that can be shared with other users), as well as their own content to add to the world (via activities like tagging, posting reviews/evaluations of content, etc.).

Libraries also need to take care with their own tools to make evident and intuitive what actions are possible with them, and what situations are appropriate to each action. For example, many academic libraries find they need constantly to explain to users that they cannot search the catalog for a topic and find journal articles; also, the "Search this Website" link on many libraries does not search for specific articles or books, although users attempt to do so. These situations have much in common with basic game design mechanics, where the range of user actions and their effects are carefully crafted so that they advance users through gameplay-like scenarios and create a clear feedback loop to guide users toward the correct path for successful task completion.

One of the keys to good feedback is that "it has to be a circle of no consequence: What you're doing in here [the game] doesn't matter outside of it, so it's okay to fail. You're forgiven" (Hinton 2006). In games, failure is often accompanied by hints as to what course of action a user should take—in a fantasy role-playing game, for example, a user might attack a certain type of creature with a sword whose powers are fire based. If the creature is resistant to fire attacks, this attack would fail, possibly resulting in the death of the character. Most game players would analyze the feedback they got from the game (a weapon doing no damage) and try a different weapon the next time around. This provides a good analogy for libraries designing information worlds for users: they need to first make it clear what "weapons" (e.g., search tools) are available, and then create interfaces that give users the right kind of feedback to know that their weapon has been ineffective and they need to try another for a better result.

GAMING AS A TOOL FOR COLLABORATION

One of the key tenets of the Library 2.0 concept is that libraries take on a more collaborative relationship with their users. This is also a key feature of modern gaming, and much can be learned from looking at how the social networks and environments built up around games support learning and goal achievement. Social networks are integral components of some types of games, such as Massive Multiplayer Online Games like World of Warcraft, in which players not only participate cooperatively to compete in game quests and goals, but can also create formal social units ("guilds") to aid in advancing in the game. WoW guilds "are formed to make grouping and raiding easier and more rewarding, as well as to form a social atmosphere in which to enjoy the game" (Guild 2006). Guilds in WoW provide support to players accomplishing difficult tasks, as "[a]ccess to fellow guild members' knowledge is a crucial part of one's own success in the game, since it is the communities' 'collective intelligence' that constitutes the most accurate and complete (living) 'strategy guide' for a given title," as well as establishing and maintaining social norms for interactions amongst players (Steinkuehler and Williams 2006).

As players participate socially to learn about game worlds and overcoming specific in-game obstacles, they become part of a network of what Gee calls "distributed knowledge." In this network, the knowledge of the group about a particular game is spread out amongst all the players of the game, and accessed through social interactions and shared guides, often known as "walkthroughs" or simply FAQs. Game knowledge thus becomes social, and even though parts of that knowledge may reside outside of an individual's physical body/mind, it is in a place (e.g., an Internet gaming site) where they can access it as needed (Gee 2003).

Much of this readily translates to the growth of Library 2.0, which is "about encouraging and enabling a library's community of users to participate, contributing their own views on resources they have used and new ones to which they might want access" (Chad and Miller 2005). We already provide "walkthroughs" of a sort through tools like research guides and pathfinders, but much of this work is still done in a monolithic and hierarchical model where the librarian as "expert" tutors the user as uninformed "newbie." In effect, we are often supplying the equivalent of the rulebooks that come with games, which many users (experienced or not) will ignore initially as they seek to learn a game through actual play. What gamers' experience suggests is that by establishing tools and methods for peer-to-peer creation and transfer of knowledge, not only does the overall group knowledge of a system increase, but newbies coming into a system have a much more robust and responsive support system to help get them past obstacles to higher levels. Librarians in this model become a sort of higher level character in the information-seeking game, who are sought out to relate their experiences in overcoming specific and consistent obstacles that newer players face. Many possibilities exist for opening up these kinds of relationships, such as allowing tagging in catalogs, creating wikis, blogs, and other tools that allow users to construct their own guides to research, and, in academic and school environments, working collaboratively with instructors within information environments to share subject and research knowledge amongst students.

CONCLUSION

Libraries today have the opportunity to reconceptualize themselves as a type of game world, wherein library users are the players and developing information seeking and critical thinking skills is part of the play. As Hawkins and Brynko (2006) note, "[v]ideo games are not about gaming, but about how people use content. By studying their example, we can understand how the real world receives information." What the growing field of gaming research has shown libraries is that the principles of learning seen in games, and the communities and peer collaboration that grow up around them, can be useful in and of themselves as the academic community designs teaching and learning environments for the next generation of student. Libraries, which share many of these same goals in the creation of their own social spaces and research environments, must in a sense become good game designers as they craft the new world of Library 2.0 collaboratively with their users.

Part of that leadership role will be releasing some of the control libraries have traditionally held onto over their information architecture, and instead of devoting resources to trying to guess how users will want to use library systems, finding ways to encourage users to create their own cheat codes, shortcuts, and mods (modifications to existing systems that allow for expanded gameplay), and design their own walk-throughs that can be shared with others. Library systems don't necessarily need to play as games in order to incorporate the methods and modes of learning that occur in games, but they do need to examine game design issues like providing timely and useful feedback to users, creating tools that allow users to measure individual success at "in-game" tasks, and constructing instructional sessions and materials that can be modified and distributed amongst users.

Finally, gaming is an activity, a medium, a method, and even a lifestyle for millions of people. But for most gamers, it is only one among many such things that comprise the totality of how they learn about and interact with the world. As such, libraries should also approach gaming as one tool for learning and education, whose methods and tools will be most effective when combined with other teaching techniques and learning principles.

REFERENCES

Bocanegra, Leti M. and Margie Harrison-Smith. "The Agricultural Economics Challenge: An Online Program where High School Students Learn Economics and Agriculture of the Salinas Valley." *First Monday (Online)* 10, no. 6 (2005). http://www.firstmonday.org/issues/issue10_6/bocanegra/index.html (retrieved November 7, 2006).

Branston, Christy. "From Game Studies to Bibliographic Gaming: Libraries Tap into the Video Game Culture." *Bulletin of the American Society for Information Science and Technology* 32, no. 4 (April/May 2006): 24–29. http://www.asis.org/Bulletin/Apr-06/branston.html (retrieved November 7, 2006).

Calore, Michael. "Web 2.0 Replaces Music Teachers." *Wired News,* November 9, 2006. http://www.wired.com/news/technology/072092-0.html?tw=wn_index_4 (retrieved November 9, 2006).

Carless, Simon. "Library of Congress Discusses Video Game Preservation." *Gamasutra,* May 3, 2006. http://www.gamasutra.com/php-bin/news_index.php?story=9156 (retrieved November 7, 2006).

Chad, Ken and Paul Miller. *Do Libraries Matter? The Rise of Library 2.0.* 2005. http://www.talis.com/downloads/white_papers/DoLibrariesMatter.pdf (retrieved November 7, 2006).

Conry-Murray, Andrew. "$18 Billion." *Network Computing* 17, no. 10 (May 25, 2006): 18.

Edwards, Cliff. "EA's Dynamic Ad Blitz." *Business Week Online,* September 8, 2006. http://www.businessweek.com/technology/content/sep2006/tc20060901_269532.htm?chan=top+news_top+news+index_technology (retrieved November 7, 2006).

ESA (Entertainment Software Association). *Facts and Research: Top 10 Industry Facts,* 2006. http://www.theesa.com/facts/top_10_facts.php (retrieved November 7, 2006).

Foreman, Joel. "Game-Based Learning: How to Delight and Instruct in the 21st Century." *Educause Review* 39, no. 5 (2004): 51–66.

Fortugno, Nick and Eric Zimmerman. "Soapbox: Learning to Play to Learn—Lessons in Educational Game Design." *Gamasutra.com,* April 5, 2005. http://www.gamasutra.com/features/20050405/zimmerman_01.shtml (retrieved November 7, 2006).

Foster, Andrea L. "Harvard to Offer Law Course in 'Virtual World.'" *Chronicle of Higher Education* 53, no. 3 (September 8, 2006): 38.

Gallaway, Beth and Alissa Lauzon. "I Can't Dance without Arrows: Getting Active @ your library with Video Game Programs." *YALS* 4, no. 4 (2006): 20–25.

Gee, James Paul. *What Video Games Have to Teach Us about Learning and Literacy.* New York: Palgrave/Macmillan, 2003.

"Grand Theft Education." *Harper's Magazine* 313, no. 1876 (2006): 30–39.

"Guild." *WowWiki,* September 26, 2006. http://www.wowwiki.com/Guild (retrieved November 7, 2006).

Gupta, Shankar. "Women Account for Two-Thirds of Online Gamers." *Online Media Daily,* October 5, 2006. http://publications.mediapost.com/index.cfm?fuseaction=Articles.san&=49247&Nid=24031&=391119 (retrieved November 7, 2006).

Gutsche, Betha. "Carvers Bay (SC) Branch Library: Gaming the Way to Literacy." *WebJunction,* September 14, 2006. http://www.webjunction.org/do/DisplayContent?id=13796 (retrieved November 7, 2006).

Hawkins, Donald T. and Barbara Brynko. "Gaming: the Next Hot Technology for Libraries?" *Information Today* 23, no. 6 (2006): 1, 51.

Hinton, Andrew. "We Live Here: Games, Third Places, and the Information Architecture of the Future." *Bulletin of the American Society for Information Science and Technology* 32, no. 6 (2006): 17–21.

Hof, Robert D. "My Virtual Life." *Business Week* 3982 (May 1, 2006): 72–82.

Jana, Reena. "Starwood Hotels Explore Second Life First." *Business Week Online,* October 12, 2006. http://www.businessweek.com/innovate/content/aug2006/id20060823_925270.htm?chan=innovation_innovation+%2B+design_innovation+and+design+lead (retrieved November 7, 2006).

Jones, Steve. "Let the Games Begin: Gaming Technology and Entertainment among College Students." *Pew Internet and American Life Project,* July 6, 2003. http://www.pewinternet.org/pdfs/PIP_College_Gaming_Reporta.pdf (retrieved November 7, 2006).

Kirriemuir, John. "From Dewey to World of Warcraft: Libraries and Digital Games." *Presentation at TICER course Digital Libraries a la Carte: New Choices for the Future*, August 25, 2006. http://www.ticer.nl/06carte/publicat/15Kirriemuir.ppt (retrieved November 7, 2006).

Kirriemuir, John and Angela McFarlane. "Literature Review in Games and Learning." *Futurelab Series*, Report 8, October 26, 2006. http://www.futurelab.org.uk/research/reviews/08_01.htm (retrieved November 7, 2006).

LaMonica, Martin. "IBM breaks ground in Second Life." *Cnet News.com* IBM Blog, October 19, 2006. http://news.com.com/2061=10809_3-6127448.html (retrieved November 7, 2006).

Lubell, Sam. "Bringing the Oldies to Modern Gamers." *New York Times*, January 30, 2003, section G, p. 6.

MacKenzie, Ann Haley. "The Brain, the Biology Classroom & Kids with Video Games." *The American Biology Teacher* 67, no. 9 (2005): 517–518.

"A Model Economy." *Economist* 374, no. 8410 (2005): 73.

Morissey, Brian. "Pontiac Drives Into Second Life." *Adweek.com*, October 23, 2006. http://www.adweek.com/aw/iq_interactive/article_display.jsp?vnu_content_id=1003286949 (retrieved November 7, 2006).

"Not Playing Around: Scientists Say Video Games Can Reshape Education." *Cnn.com*, October 17, 2006. http://www.cnn.com/2006/EDUCATION/10/17/video.games.ap/index.html (retrieved November 7, 2006).

Olsen, Stefanie. "Are Virtual Worlds the Future of the Classroom?" *CNet News.com*, June 12, 2006. http://news.com.com/2009-1041_3-6081870.html (retrieved November 7, 2006).

Scalzo, John. "The Video Game Librarian: Six Months Later." *Gaming Target*, June 24, 2005. http://www.gamingtarget.com/article.php?artid=4411 (retrieved November 7, 2006).

Shreve, Jenn. "Let the Games Begin: Video Games, Once Confiscated in Class, Are Now a Key Teaching Tool. If They're Done Right." *Edutopia* (April 2005): 29–31. http://www.edutopia.org/magazine/ed1article.php?id&=Art_1268&issue=apr_05 (retrieved November 7, 2006).

Steinkuehler, Constance and Dmitri Williams. "Where Everybody Knows Your (Screen) Name: Online Games as 'Third Places.'" *Journal of Computer-Mediated Communication* 11, no. 4 (2006): article 1. http://jcmc.indiana.edu/vol11/issue4/steinkuehler.html (retrieved November 7, 2006).

Stephens, Michael. "Promoting Gaming Programs in Libraries." *Information Today* 20, no. 2 (2006). http://www.infotoday.com/MLS/mar06/Stephens.shtml (retrieved November 7, 2006).

Sutton, Lynn and David H. Womack. "Got Game?" *C RL News* 67, no. 3 (2006): 173–176.

Taub, Eric A. "Nintendo Courts the Gray Gamer." *CNet News.com*, October 30, 2006. http://news.com.com/Nintendo+courts+the+gray+gamer/2100-1043_3-6130590.html (retrieved November 7, 2006).

Terdiman, Daniel. "Reuters' 'Second Life' Reporter Talks Shop." *Cnet News.com*, October 26, 2006. http://news.com.com/Reuters+Second+Life+reporter+talks+shop/2008-1043_3-6129335.html (retrieved November 7, 2006).

Trotter, Andrew. "Digital Games Bring Entertainment into Learning Realm." *Education Week* 23, no. 44 (August 11, 2004): 8.

Van Eck, Richard. "Digital Game-Based Learning: It's Not Just the Digital Natives Who Are Restless." *EDUCAUSE Review* 41, no. 2 (2006): 16–30.

Whelan, Debra Lau. "Let the Games Begin!" *School Library Journal* 51, no. 4 (April 1, 2005): 40–43.

10

LIBRARY 2.0 AND VIRTUAL WORLDS = INNOVATION + EXPLORATION

Lori Bell, Tom Peters, and Kitty Pope

Libraries in the twenty-first century ... Library 2.0 ... Web 2.0 ... Everything 2.0 ... Innovation is both a keyword and a mission-critical trend for corporations, businesses, nonprofit organizations, and libraries. Organizations of all types are realizing the need to explore new online environments and social software tools. The evolution of the web, from passing static text only in 1995 to graphical, dynamic web content and mashups, is becoming more and more interactive to engage users and involve them in the processes of using and creating information. Static web pages, no matter how attractive, are no longer enough to impress users of the next generation, or perhaps any generation using the Internet. Much emphasis is placed on how to educate, how to engage, how to get those under 35 and especially teens, to purchase, attend, or engage in an activity, including the library.

The need to innovate, explore, and engage users is truly becoming very important to businesses, education, and libraries, but the emphasis on the younger generation could be a red herring. Most surveys and studies confirm that the use of the Internet is on the rise across all age categories, especially older adults. In his blog Stephen's Lighthouse, Stephen Abram, Vice President of Innovation for SirsiDynix, describes a definition of Web 2.0 as "Web 2.0 is all the websites out there that get their value from the actions of users." How users respond to and use the information delivered by libraries is as important as the information itself.

In this chapter we will explore libraries and virtual worlds, especially a project spearheaded by the Alliance Library System (ALS) to create a library presence in the virtual world of Second Life. ALS, located in East Peoria, Illinois, is one of nine multitype regional library systems in Illinois. The four core services of ALS are continuing education, consulting, delivery, and resource sharing for its 259 member libraries of all types. In 2006 Executive Director Kitty Pope created a new Department of Innovation to assist member libraries in finding grants and other alternative funding, organize collaborative projects, and help libraries innovate.

In the Alliance Library System Trends Report for 2006, Ms. Pope discussed the concept and importance of innovation for libraries seeking to thrive and grow in the twenty-first century. The concept of innovation—changing things to make programs operate better or more efficiently—is not new, but the pace of innovation in the twenty-first century already is accelerating at a rapid rate. In her annual *Trends Report* (2006) for the Alliance board of directors, Ms. Pope wrote, "innovation is the buzz word of 2006!" She also wrote that research indicates the companies that focus on innovation have consistently higher profit margins than those that do not. Some of the most innovative companies in 2006 as ranked by the Boston Consulting Group (2006) are no surprise: Apple, Google, Toyota, and Microsoft. Two important factors in innovation, according to Pope, are growth and risk. It requires thinking outside the box, success, and failure. It also requires time to explore, think, and plan, which can be quite time consuming for libraries with strapped budgets and shrinking staffs.

Some of the other trends in the report and other sources indicate reduced use of bricks and mortar libraries by young adults and increased use of the Internet by people of all ages, especially older adults. Customer service trends in libraries show that more and more self-services are desired by library users, from self-check out machines to more services on the web, such as virtual reference, and collections, such as ebooks and audio books. Format changes are also affecting this trend with the increase in and popularity of digital audio books including downloadable audio books and the Playaway, a self-playing digital audio book, and an escalating popularity in gaming and participating in virtual worlds such as Second Life and There.com.

The concept of gaming, which goes back to ancient times, really covers everything from tabletop games such as checkers, cards, and Monopoly to elaborate, massively multiuser virtual games such as World of Warcraft. Gaming is another Library 2.0 key concept. Most people think more in terms of young adults playing computer games via CD-ROM or Internet. Interactive "games" on the Internet such as World of Warcraft that include players from all over the world are increasing in popularity as are the use of virtual worlds. Sometimes people think of online virtual worlds as games, but there is a difference. Games require someone to increase in skill and, as they progress, the game becomes more difficult. Virtual worlds are very similar to real life in that you can do many of the same things, such as take classes, interact with others, visit museums and libraries, gamble, and other things.

Just as during the past 30 years an increasing percentage of the world's information and communication has migrated to computer networks such as the Internet, we now seem poised to rapidly increase our human endeavors in virtual worlds. The concept of virtual worlds has been around for decades, but only now are we seeing virtual world populations grow to sizes—often more than one million residents per world—that can have a global impact on information and communication networks.

Because the use of many public libraries by young adults in the ALS geographic region has been declining, ALS staff wrote several grant applications to coordinate gaming activity in some of its member libraries in order to increase young adult use. These grants were not funded and staff began to wonder if grant readers understood the important relationship between gaming, learning, and literacy.

At the Gaming and Learning Symposium held in Chicago by the Metropolitan Library System in December 2005, ALS staff member Lori Bell learned about libraries offering gaming activities and increasing services and use by young adults because of the gaming activity. Virtual worlds and education were also discussed at this symposium, so ALS staff and consultant Tom Peters began investigating how virtual worlds such as Active Worlds, There.com, and Second Life were being used by libraries and education.

Two academic libraries—Appalachian State University and Eastern University in Pennsylvania—had established strong and successful library presences in campus-specific use of Active Worlds where the institution's faculty were also teaching classes. ALS staff visited and assessed both libraries online. Appalachian State's virtual world library tended to focus on a few specific disciplines whereas Eastern University's library seemed to have a broader focus and resources. Both were attractive and well-developed libraries with extensive information resources. ALS staff members were impressed with both institutions and spoke to staff at Appalachian State. There, students seemed to enjoy interacting with librarians in the virtual world, but staff involved indicated it was time-consuming to staff a physical institution, virtual reference services, and the Active Worlds presence in the evenings.

The findings of this investigation compared similarly to virtual reference projects in which Peters and Bell had been involved. The ideal virtual or web-based reference service, even offered by individual institutions, should be available all the time. Most libraries are challenged to staff a physical reference desk for the hours the library is open, much less 24/7. As virtual reference services have evolved from asynchronous e-mail to synchronous chat and involvement grows by libraries of all types and sizes, the majority of libraries are joining statewide and global consortia to be able to offer the service 24/7. Through collaboration of this type, both the burden and the risk of an always-available service are spread over all the participating libraries.

Peters and Bell then visited Second Life. They had read several articles in Second Life publications and on the Internet about a Second Life Public Library. Pictures of the library revealed a typical but beautiful modern library building on the coast of an ocean. "Jade Lily" (Second Life name) started the library and developed the concept. For some reason, the library never took off and the building it was in was no longer available. Other libraries in Second Life were identified, but received limited or no use or appeared abandoned. Some were very special, narrow subject libraries. An excellent black library was also identified that was an extension of a website (http://www.alwaysblack.com). Books took the user out to works on the website. The library was in an attractive building and also had games and comic books. Again, it was a specialized library.

WHAT IS SECOND LIFE?

Second Life is a virtual world entirely built and owned by its residents, who often are called "avatars." Participants build an avatar, or alternate persona, to participate actively in the creation of media instead of the more passive modes of watching television, or viewing a static web page. The Wikipedia article "Avatar (icon)" provides some historical context about the use of the Hindu concept of avatars to name the residents of virtual environments.

Since opening to the public in 2003, Second Life has grown explosively, and today is inhabited by more than 1.3 million people from around the globe. New participants discover a vast digital continent and hundreds of islands and archipelagos, teeming with people, entertainment, and opportunities. After exploring, individuals might decide to buy land, purchase a home, or start a business. They will also be surrounded by the creations of fellow residents. Because residents retain the rights to their digital creations, they can buy, sell, and trade with other residents. Second Life even has its own currency—Linden Dollars—which can be converted to U.S. Dollars and other real-world currencies. Everything you can imagine (and some you cannot) can be found in Second Life. There are museums, nineteenth-century worlds where residents dress in period clothing and live in Victorian homes, immersive learning environments such as an Egyptian tomb, Star Trek futuristic realms, a replica of the French Quarter in New Orleans, and much more. Residents can go to the virtual library and use a number of resources.

Although some might view virtual environments as new and unproven, in fact online communities often provide new environments for mutual support and learning, in some ways embodying the evolving roles of libraries within their "real life" communities. Student use of academic libraries is decreasing with the advent of the Internet and online resources, causing these institutions to rethink the nature of collections, services, and the library as real-world places. As college campuses, hospitals, and other educational and nonprofit institutions investigate and establish their presence in virtual worlds such as Second Life and Active Worlds (e.g., Appalachian State University and Eastern University in Pennsylvania), it was deemed important to explore a virtual world library presence for the 259 multitype member libraries in the ALS. In April 2006, Alliance started a library in Second Life to investigate library services in the virtual world. Immediately, Alliance was approached by a number of other partners to provide library services and to work with organizations to develop customized resources for specific educational programs.

The demographics of people using Second Life are surprising. The average age is 35, approximately 50 percent female and 50 percent male, and about 60 percent of users are from the United States. Among the United States-based Second Life population, the East Coast is as well-represented as the West Coast. In late summer 2006 it became possible to get a free account without providing a credit card or cell phone number that made it much easier for people from other countries to participate.

BUILDING A SECOND LIFE LIBRARY

Unable to locate any library that was a regular library such as an academic or public library, and fascinated and intrigued by the endless facets of the virtual world of Second Life, in April 2006, Bell proposed the idea of a virtual world library to Kitty Pope. Enthusiastic about the idea, Pope provided Bell with seed money for such an experiment from funds collected through a fundraising project. Bell invited anyone interested in collaborating to join in the effort that was first a small prefabricated building on a small plot of land in Second Life. Very quickly, an excited volunteer force of librarians from across the United States and throughout the world formed to work with Alliance to discover if residents in a virtual world really wanted and needed a library. Also very quickly, the group found that innovation requires exploration and exploration is quite time consuming. Most of the original volunteers for the project worked for the Alliance Second Life Library on their own time because most supervisors were not sure that a virtual world did not equal a game. Was the work they were doing serving the tax base of patrons they were paid to serve? Pope was generous with work time for the project, but the new Department of Innovation with one staff member also had a number of other projects that were important.

The first library, a "pre-fab," which looked like a traditional library, was soon joined by a medical library managed by Namro Orman (SL name), a Dutch medical librarian. The number of volunteers continued to grow and the group began working on a business plan with interested citizens.

CHALLENGES

The challenges in attempting to build a virtual library in Second Life have been many. First and foremost, living in a virtual world is like living on another planet that is similar to Planet Earth in some ways, and markedly different in other ways. Simply moving around is a challenge and learning how to move about with grace and aplomb takes time. Even though one can fly, it takes time to learn how to do so without bumping into other people, walls, buildings, and falling to the ground with arms flailing. As in other countries, there are certain rules of etiquette, ways of doing things, and ways of not doing things. It is possible to teleport one's avatar a la Star Trek. There are also holodecks where one can select the scenery of their surroundings.

In a virtual world, someone may or may not be who they say they are, just as elsewhere on the Internet. One needs to learn certain skills or find someone who does or pay for those skills. For example, some of our volunteers could build beautiful things, some could script or program computers. Some were better at doing reference or planning programs or events.

The learning curve to live in Second Life is high and it is time consuming as it is in most virtual worlds. Even when one plans to work or spend only one hour, often one ends up being in-world five or six hours because it is so fascinating and there are so many interesting things to see and do.

Another challenge was that many people came to the library expecting expertise on the culture from us. Most of us working in the Second Life Library were newbies ourselves and therefore unable to provide much assistance. After 6 months we are now much more able to help people or point them to the right direction.

THE DIGITAL DIVIDE

The technical requirements for a computer and graphics card to access Second Life are high—again as with the advent of the Internet or any new technology, there is the digital divide. Those who use Second Life have to have broadband Internet access and with the technical requirements many people may not be able to access Second Life. The digital divide is something librarians try to address on a consistent basis but, with the rapid change in technologies of the twenty-first century, may never totally bridge. In April 2006, when the Alliance Second Life Library was first formed, there were approximately 180,000 residents of Second Life. By early November 2006, there were over 1.3 million residents.

EDUCATION AND CORPORATIONS

Although not everyone agrees about the value and importance of virtual worlds, and although virtual worlds are not for everyone, libraries need to be there. Higher education is moving into worlds like Second Life and Active Worlds at a rapid pace. Over 100 educational institutions are offering classes in Second Life as an alternative or supplement to Blackboard, WebCT, and other common distance learning packages. A major component of Library 2.0 is going where the users are, and the number of users in virtual worlds is increasing. Many major corporations are also making the move into Second Life including IBM, Nature Magazine, Pontiac, Infinite Mind Radio Station, and Penguin Publishers. Who knows what the dominant future virtual world will be—Active Worlds, Second Life, Google Earth? However, there is no doubt this is where education, corporate activity, and some library activity is going.

STAFFING

Staffing a "volunteer" library has and will continue to be a challenge for the Second Life Library. Traditional libraries may be open 12 hours a day; the Second Life Library is global in nature and is open 24/7 although it is not always staffed. Many businesses and shops in Second Life are not staffed at all and are completely self-service. One sees what one wants, clicks on it, and makes a purchase. The library is often unstaffed, not because it is viewed as unimportant, but because there are not enough volunteers available to staff 24/7. The library is staffed a few hours a day at the welcome desk and is using an OCLC QuestionPoint trial to answer e-mail questions when a librarian is not there, and chat within QuestionPoint and the chat and instant message feature in Second Life to answer questions when a librarian is on duty.

Staffing the library in a virtual world is very important. In our case, it is not a click-and-buy operation. Building resources that are scattered first across one and now four islands requires that the library should provide instruction, orientation, and reference service. Response to this has been very positive, especially from new people. The library attracts a lot of new residents who receive a warm welcome and maybe even directions to a teleport they are looking for. They are told where to buy clothes, where to go to hear good music, and about library programs that might appeal to them. We even mention real-world library resources when appropriate to the avatar's information need. Although the library is global and there are volunteers from many countries, the library tends to be busiest during the early to late evening hours in the continental United States. Since many librarians cannot come on during the day because their supervisors do not understand or because the library is already strapped for staffing its bricks and mortar presence, more librarians are available at night—and more people tend to be on at night.

The library is a collaborative effort as are many virtual reference projects. By volunteering a staff member a few hours per week to this project, a library is able to experiment and participate in the virtual world library, with less risk and less money. Working collaboratively, there is a greater amount of expertise on different subjects, and the opportunity for librarians to meet others—librarians and patrons from all over the country and the world.

EVENTS

Second Life Library hosts a number of events just as libraries do in real life. Several authors from real life, including the writing team of Steven Miller and Sharon Lee, have spoken about how they got started writing and built a group of fans from the early days of the Internet. They write and publish science fiction books in real life and have a presence in Second Life where they offer snippets of their books. Sharon Woodward and Wilbur Witt, another husband-wife writing team, spoke at a well-attended program on their book entitled *Dobbit Do*, which was published in real life and Second Life. J. C. Hutchins, who writes a series called 7th Son, a scifi thriller that is podcast into a podiobook (a series of audio files from the book as podcasts), shared his work with almost 50 attendees and then gave a tour of several scenes from his book set up in Second Life. As in real life, the Second Life Library wants to support the authors, writers, and creativity and works of its citizens.

The Library has also had a number of programs on technology efforts happening in Second Life. Jeff Barr, a technology evangelist at Amazon.com, talked to a group about the technology Amazon.com is working with and how they are using it to create a presence in Second Life. Lex Lardner (SL name), who works with Jnana technology on the web in the real world, is giving this free to those in Second Life who wish to work with it to provide information in an interactive fashion. He provided a program to a packed house.

As many real life libraries do, the Second Life Library has a monthly book discussion program where Maxito Ricardo (SL name) leads the discussion of a variety of different titles and genres. Not many people have attended these, but we are hoping attendance will pick up.

Library staff have also provided a number of tours and training sessions for Second Life Library residents and students. Leading avatars on a tour is like trying to herd cats that can fly and teleport at will. Central Missouri State University has a professor who teaches entire classes in Second Life. The staff worked with him to provide library tours and assistance to his class of writing students. The staff is currently working with the New Media Consortium (NMC) campus that has 200 university and museum members to provide library services—materials, tours, and orientations for any interested faculty member.

Recently, the Second Life Library Staff formed a continuing education group focused on three areas—to provide programs and library training to residents and students in Second life; to provide training on Second Life skills to new residents; and to provide continuing education and professional development for the librarians in Second Life.

One of the most popular programs the library has offered are training skills on how to do things in Second Life, such as how to improve your avatar, to build a building, to do scripting, and so forth. Eiseldora Reisman (SL name) has provided leadership in this area. She is a recent library school graduate and has ten to twenty people in each class who appreciate her time and skills.

EXHIBITS

Among the most popular activities the library has offered have been different types of exhibits. The Illinois State Library provided materials to Second Life Library staff from its Vachel Lindsay collection. Staff set up period furniture and used photographs from the collection with the furniture to create a Lindsay feel to the room. By clicking on a picture, residents could listen to a poem written by Lindsay or read the text of others. The Illinois State Library also had an excellent World War II collection, which was presented in Second Life and enjoyed by many who might not have had the opportunity to see the collection if they had not visited the Second Life Library. ALS used photographs and audio descriptions (an audio in-depth description of a photograph for someone who is visually impaired) to provide access to information and photographs of a nineteenth-century opera singer from Peoria, Illinois, and an early female physician from Quincy, Illinois. Textual biographical information was also provided. The Science Center of the library recently developed an excellent exhibit where one could experience a certain type of color blindness; they could view the room in its "normal" state and then as if they had the vision problem. The Science Center just started its organization and activity in October 2006, and is planning some more exhibits.

During the summer 2006, the Library of Congress gave Second Life Library permission to use its materials on the Declaration of Independence at the virtual library. Shadow Fugazi (SL name) created a beautiful exhibit with graphics on the men who signed the document, images of the documents themselves, and audio reading of the document. This exhibit was well received and we hope is the first of many. We are also working on ways to create more immersive and interactive exhibits to make them more lifelike.

FROM TRADITIONAL TO VIRTUAL

In building the Second Life Library during the first 6 months, we started with what was familiar—something similar to a traditional library. Often when people visit for the first time they are disappointed because what they see may look to them like a traditional library. The materials, exhibits, and programs can be very different though. We are trying to build on what we know to create something new—a library for the twenty-first century in a virtual world. We are limited by the tools provided to do this by Linden Labs, which owns Second Life, the knowledge of those involved, which is increasing as we gain more experience, and time. Creating anything in Second Life—be it a building or an exhibit—is very time intensive.

We will only get better as we grow. One of the questions we hope to answer as this project progresses is what services should a virtual library provide? Should they be the same as in the real world, should they be different, are there new services? At the 6-month point we think there are some services and materials that will remain the same and some that will be better—with the use of new technologies. Then again, it may look nothing like we think of libraries today. We wish we had a crystal ball.

HEALTHINFO ISLAND

During the fall 2006, ALS received a grant from the National Library of Medicine Greater Midwest Region to create health resources and share them in Second Life. An island was purchased called HealthInfo Island and the medical library and a new consumer health library were moved to that island. Staff will work with support groups, many of which also exist in real life, to create and provide needed resources. Staff will also offer training on how to use Medline Plus and other consumer health resources and how to evaluate the information found.

CRITICISM AND PRAISE

Like all new projects employing new technology, Second Life Library has received its share of praise and criticism. From, "this is the wow of the year" to "people working on this stuff should be fired," we have read and heard it all. With the proliferation of blogs, there has been tremendous discussion on this effort, some helpful, some hurtful, much constructive. Although it is not for everyone, there is something for everyone who wants to become involved. No one is good at everything, yet everyone can contribute something even if they feel they are not good at technology. We urge volunteers to limit the time they spend in-world. We have lost a number of wonderful volunteers to self-inflicted burnout.

MENTORSHIP/OPPORTUNITIES

One of the greatest opportunities for the Second Life Library has been the global participation. Participants meet and work with librarians from all over the world and encounter people they might never have had the opportunity to meet. It also offers opportunities for librarians, whether right out of library school or of any age, to innovate, create, try a new service, and get some experience with the technology.

CYBRARY CITY

During the summer of 2006 the Alliance Second Life Library won second place in the Talis Library Mashup Competition. The Library received a great deal of publicity and some prize money for the award. Prize money was used to purchase new buildings and furniture for the library. During fall 2006, Talis agreed to sponsor Cybrary City right next to Info Island. Cybrary City is an island created for librarians with a conference and training center and a small place for each library to claim as its own to feature local collections or information or simply for their librarians working on Info Island to have a place to meet. The only thing required to have a spot is to contribute 2 hours per week to the collaborative Info Island as a whole.

CONCLUSION

We already have the answer to our most pressing question: do people/avatars want library services in a virtual world? The answer is a resounding yes. The number of visits continues to increase as does attendance at programs. The most challenging issues are continuing to fund and staff a volunteer-run library, the number of hours a number of staff are putting in, training new volunteers in the skills they need, not for the library portion, but the Second Life portion, and determining what are the most desired services in a virtual world. Another concern is that Second Life is experiencing phenomenal growth now, but how long will this last? We cannot take the items we create in Second Life to another virtual world. We will have learned skills we can take to another world, but what will be the virtual world or operating system of choice in the end? We hope we will not have wasted our time and efforts in this endeavor. As people of all ages spend more and more time on the Internet and in virtual worlds, they still want and need libraries.

REFERENCES

Alliance Library System. *2006 Trends Report*, June 8, 2006. http://www.alliancelibrarysystem. com/pdf/Trends2006.pdf (retrieved December 4, 2006).
Boston Consulting Group. "Innovative Companies Build Innovation Cultures." *Tekrati*, May 4, 2006. http://www.tekrati.com/research/News.asp?id=6890 (retrieved December 4, 2006).

11

DIGITAL STORYTELLING, LIBRARIES, AND COMMUNITY

Karen Diaz and Anne M. Fields

The word "storytelling" connotes something primitive, even childlike. It brings to mind sitting around a campfire being delightfully frightened by a ghost story, or sitting on a rug in kindergarten listening to classmates show and tell. Therefore, a chapter on storytelling in a book on next-generation library technologies may seem anachronistic. But for centuries cultures of all kinds have used stories to construct themselves. Libraries have become a crucial part of cultural construction by collecting, preserving, and sharing cultures' stories. A digital story is simply a story told using some combination of still and moving digital images, digital voiceover narrative, and digital music. Digital storytelling has empowered people in a variety of settings to tell their personal stories. We believe it can empower libraries, as well, to move into building deeper relationships with our communities, both internal and external.

Digital stories are a kind of social networking technology not unlike blogs and wikis that allow storytellers and their audiences to share mutually interesting content through the use of new digital technologies. After all, what is more social than sharing stories with others, stories about our children, stories about our bosses, stories about our football teams? Yet digital stories usually are not included on lists of social networking technologies, perhaps because they simply are not yet as well known as other more popular technologies or because often we may be calling them by another name or not calling them by a name at all. What differentiates digital stories—as we will define them—from some of the other technologies discussed in *Library 2.0*, however, is their necessarily affective nature. The shared emotion generated between teller and listener by a well-told story draws people together in ways that the unimodal and frequently unedited character of blogs and wikis may not.

STORIES IN SOCIETY

Individuals, families, tribes, and peoples have been telling stories for as long as memory reaches, organizing the details of their experience in order to remember and capture their histories and to shape their identities. By organizing that experience they make sense of it. They articulate life lessons and shared values. Civic, academic, religious, ethnic, national, and even corporate cultures all have stories to tell. From the story of the founders of small towns or colleges, to stories of the origin of the universe or the cycles of the seasons, the heroes of 9/11, and even the story of Dave Thomas, founder of Wendy's, and his own youth as an orphan—all these stories form part of the identities of particular cultures. In the early twenty-first century, as academic libraries seem in danger of becoming increasingly irrelevant to the institutions they serve, the stories of library history, treasures, and people offer libraries opportunities to become not just collectors of stories but storytellers in their own right, reviving their own spirits and connecting with their communities.

Storytelling is a reciprocal process of give and take between storytellers and their audiences. Through humor or pathos, tension or suspense, storytellers engage with their audiences. The storyteller reaches out through the story; the listener responds with a laugh, a tear, a gasp, a nod of recognition or agreement. That engagement builds community and, some claim, in turn develops the moral sense by putting the listener "in the throes of a story" and "by allowing you to project yourself into the lives of people of different times and places and races" (Pinker and Goldstein 2004, paragraphs 28–31).

A NEW ROLE FOR STORIES IN SOCIETY

In his book *A Whole New Mind*, Daniel Pink writes that we are moving from the Information Age with its "logical, linear, computerlike capabilities" to the Conceptual Age that, he argues, is an "economy and a society built on the inventive, empathetic, big-picture capabilities" (Pink 2005, 1–2). Recent discoveries about the duality of left- and right-brained-thinking are unseating previous assumptions that sequential, literal, textual, and analytic thinking are the sole drivers of human information processing. This shift has made room for new partners exemplified by metaphorical, aesthetic, contextual, and synthetic thinking. The Conceptual Age does not invalidate the left brain but rather partners left-brained with right-brained thinking.

Pink asserts that one of the abilities that will help individuals excel in the Conceptual Age is story. When Pink talks of "story," he refers to the fact that stories provide context for facts. That is, people can recount their childhoods sequentially—when they were born, where they lived, who their friends were—without providing a reason for the regurgitation of this data. But when people tell stories about their lives, adding dramatic shape and including emotional content, the mere facts gain context and meaning. Along with meaning may come empathy as listeners are better able to imagine themselves in the teller's place and time, as Pinker and Goldstein suggest (2004, paragraphs 28–31).

Applied to libraries, Pink's logic makes sense. The last 30 to 40 years have produced almost unlimited access to information. How many analysts have determined that the flow of information to the average person has removed the "gate" from the idea of "librarian as gatekeeper?" We do not even need to be facilitators any more. Instead, libraries now must be concerned with the more right-brained aptitudes of artistry, empathy, sense-making, and emotional connection. Managing information can no longer be our only occupation. We must incorporate new roles of helping users to find meaning in information, to care about it, and to develop empathy from it.

Joe Lambert of the Center for Digital Storytelling (CDS) talks of the "re-storification" of our culture. He points out that "[i]n traditional cultures, the intermingling of personal stories, communal stories, myths, legends and folktales not only entertained us, but created a powerful empathetic bond between ourselves and our communities" (Lambert 2002, xviii). Perhaps all the years of allowing the few in our society to be the storytellers with access to film and television technologies have removed an element of that communal sense of storytelling. Digital storytelling is a way of restoring voice to Everyman, allowing us to "re-story" our society. Thus, if "Library 2.0" is all about using the new technologies available to us to become more user-centered, then digital storytelling is one tool for striking up a conversation with users about who we are and what we have to offer. And if within our own organization we represent interdependent groups of "users" too, digital storytelling offers a way for us to begin to know ourselves and each other better.

ELEMENTS OF DIGITAL STORYTELLING

A digital story is a story told using some combination of digital still images, video clips, voiceover narrative, and music. In order to maintain focus, and because of file storage issues, they tend to be short—usually only 3 to 5 minutes long. If hardware and software are kept simple enough, people of all ages and walks of life can create effective digital stories.

The list of required hardware and software is relatively short:

- computer (preferably with a DVD burner)
- digital camera
- scanner
- USB microphone
- tabletop microphone stand
- photo editing software (for instance, iPhoto or Photoshop)
- sound recording software (for instance, Sound Studio, GarageBand, or Audacity)
- video editing software (for instance, iMovie or Adobe Premier)
- optional: digital video camera, headphones

Digital storytelling, as we describe it here, was conceptualized in the 1990s by the late Dana Atchley who, with Joe Lambert and Nina Mullen, went on to found the Center for Digital Storytelling (CDS) in Berkeley, CA. Today the CDS offers workshops both on- and off-site to teach people how to create digital stories and to train others to extend the center's work. The CDS has collaborated with organizations as diverse as the British Broadcasting Corporation, the National Gallery of Art, and the Kansas City Symphony.

In *Digital Storytelling: Capturing Lives, Creating Community*, Lambert lists "the seven elements" of digital storytelling:

- Point (of view)
- Dramatic question
- Emotional content
- The gift of your voice
- The power of the soundtrack
- Economy
- Pacing

Lambert conflates point and point of view to describe two different aspects of storytelling. The point of a story is the author's overall goal, or why this story is important for the author to tell at this moment in his or her life. Some of the points around which we have seen stories created are: I want you to know that I was not sure that my adopted Chinese daughter would ever love me. I want you to feel the sweetness of southern living. I want you to see how heroic my mother was. I want you to understand why a new library will mean more to me than four new walls, up-to-date computers, and miles of book stacks.

Point of view, on the other hand, is the perspective from which the author tells his story. He might consider such questions as: Am I looking back to the past or forward into the future? Am I emotionally involved with my story or more distant and objective? Am I revealing all the details, or keeping some things hidden?

The author's dramatic question brings the point of the story and its point of view into focus for the listener, keeping the listener involved from beginning to end. It may be revealed in the very first sentence of the narration or it may only be suggested by the background music or a key image. The dramatic question that warranted the delightful digital story on sweet tea was: Why is sweet tea so inextricably linked with southerners' sense of place? The dramatic question around which the story of the adopted Chinese daughter revolved was: Would my daughter ever smile for me?

The emotional content of the digital story distinguishes these stories from a mere recitation of the day's activities to a colleague or a public relations video distributed by a library's communications office. The emotion conveyed by the story can run the gamut from delight to melancholy to horror. It is one key factor in establishing connection between the storyteller and the listener. Acknowledging the emotional potential of stories and permitting those emotions to be expressed within the library environment is perhaps one of the biggest leaps that librarians have to make. With this challenge comes great potential, however, as digital stories become a tool for building community within and outside the library.

Appropriately labeled as a "gift," the teller's own voice in the digital story provides a wealth of information to the listener. Rather than listening to a neutralized voiceover actor, the listener hears a flesh and blood person whose voice suggests that she is a woman, possibly elderly, perhaps African-American, probably from somewhere in the South. Maybe it's the voice of a child, or an aging veteran. Hearing that voice the listener begins to form a picture of the storyteller that deepens and intensifies the meaning of the story being told and enriches it many times over.

Imagine *Schindler's List* without John Williams' music or *American Graffiti* without its 1950s and 1960s collage of rock and roll hits to carry you back into that era. This is the "power of the soundtrack" to which Lambert refers. Digital stories certainly can be told without music—and there may be times when the very absence of music speaks eloquently—but in general music adds another layer to the story that enhances mood, builds emotion, and even can tell part of the story. One of our colleagues, for example, is working on a digital story about swing dancing to use in a conversational English class with Chinese students. While swing music as soundtrack obviously is appropriate to the story, it also serves a practical purpose of "describing" for foreign listeners exactly what swing music is.

With usually only 3 to 5 minutes in which to tell the story—approximately 150 words—a storyteller has to be economical. He must spend every word wisely, as if each one were his last penny. Equivocation and redundancy have no place here, and everything learned in freshman composition about writing concisely comes into play. Fortunately, images and soundtrack can help the storyteller in this regard with a picture becoming literally worth a thousand words. As Lambert points out, juxtaposed images and sound provide another and richer text to be heard and interpreted by the listener (Lambert 2002, 58).

Finally, even the shortest digital video can bore its audience or waste its potential impact if the storyteller does not pace it effectively. Variation in speed, rhythm, and intensity of the narrator's voice, the music, and the presentation of images all matter. That is, does the narrator pause, does the music become louder or softer, does the story occasionally cut quickly between images or use slow fades or even some black space between them?

While the digital story format is particularly well-suited to stories about one's life outside the working world, we have come to believe that the seven elements can be incorporated into stories about libraries as well. For example, an archivist at our institution created a digital story (http://hdl.handle.net/1811/24060) about her involvement with a historical cartoon collection that demonstrated all seven of these elements. The point of the story was to make visible to the world this somewhat hidden collection. The story was told from the point of view of one who knew intimately every inch of the 716 linear feet of materials dating from 1894 to 1996 that comprised the San Francisco Academy of Comic Art Collection of newspaper comic strips purchased by Ohio State University in 1997 from collector William Blackbeard. Her dramatic question was why would I take on a task as daunting as trying to organize a collection of over 2.5 million newspaper clippings, comic pages, and newspapers? The emotion that her story clearly conveyed was her passion for preserving the cultural history embodied in these materials, yet the tone of her voice was nostalgic, with a slight Georgia lilt to it. An old piano-roll rag played in the background, establishing without words the time period of some of the more colorful comics. While she lingered on some images to lure her audience into the collection, she varied the pacing of the story by increasing the speed between cuts as she showed images of the tractor-trailers that were required to ship the collection from California to Ohio. This story not only exemplifies all seven elements of a digital story, but also exemplifies one possible application of the form in a library setting.

MAKING A DIGITAL STORY

Products like Apple's iLife suite make moviemaking technology something people can learn on their own in their own homes. There is more to making a story, however, than using the technology. To better illustrate what it takes to make a digital story, and then later highlight the challenges inherent in making future stories, we'd like to tell you the story of our own first experience with digital storytelling.

When we first read about digital storytelling we had been participating in a study group in our library that was investigating trends in teaching and learning in university classrooms and libraries. Some of our reading about learning had interested us in the notion of multimodal projects as a means for students to demonstrate their learning. It occurred to us that student projects would be apt content to display on big-screen TVs that our library was planning to install in its renovated building. It also occurred to us that library staff had an ample supply of stories that could be told multimodally and also displayed on those screens, as well as through the library's website, our institutional repository, and other venues.

We registered for a 3-day digital storytelling workshop led by the Center for Digital Storytelling in Asheville, NC, in April 2005. Most of the twelve participants planned to work individually, but a few of us worked as pairs. Participants ranged from high-school teachers, to college students, to college professors, and we two librarians. All were instructed to come prepared with a script of no more than 150 words, as well as images and music that we might want to include in our movies.

Although we knew that the CDS stresses personal digital stories, we wanted to tell a story about the 3-year renovation our main library was about to undergo. We especially wanted to talk about how the library was moving toward becoming a library that emphasizes learning over teaching and that pays attention to the university's undergraduates. We brought with us pictures of the library and the campus; a script in which we tried to incorporate faculty, student, and librarian points of view; and a Larry Carlton jazz guitar CD.

Probably the most important part of the digital storytelling workshop is the morning spent sharing the group members' scripts in a story "circle" during which each person or pair presents his or her script. The rest of the group then responds to the script commenting on what parts of the story most strongly affect them, what particularly engages their interest, or what makes them want to know more about the teller and the tale. Group members also may ask questions to guide the teller's revisions, such as: Why did you especially want to tell this story; or, what's the one thing you remember best about this person you're telling about?

Our group's subjects ranged from the weighty (a mother's transport to a Nazi concentration camp) to the sentimental (a thirtieth wedding anniversary) to the humorous (sweetened iced tea). Even at that early stage in the workshop and without digital embellishment several stories drew tears. Our turn came last. Compared to everyone else's, our script—related to our professional lives—was businesslike and lifeless, and we knew it. We were only grateful that no one laughed.

"If you really want to write about the library," Joe Lambert drawled, "I suppose that's all right. But I'd be interested in knowing what all these changes mean to you personally." We spent the whole evening thinking not about the library's story but our own story, and by the next morning we had transformed our script completely.

The next 2 days were a whirlwind of scanning photographs, learning photo and video editing applications, recording our scripts, and laying down our musical soundtracks. The workshop culminated nearly 3 hectic days after we had begun with showing all the final digital stories to each other. Almost everyone had taken comments from the story circle to heart and incorporated them into their final movies, often with dramatic results. A slight change in focus of the script, lingering on a particular photograph, or varying background music to change the tempo of the pacing brought remarkable poignancy to many of the stories that, only 2 days before, had been unfocused and incoherent. We had traveled to Asheville simply curious about the process of creating digital stories, but we returned home convinced that the form promised to allow the library to tell its stories in ways we had not anticipated.

While we returned from Asheville having created our own story, we did not return expert enough to run such a workshop ourselves. Several months later we brought Joe Lambert to our own campus to do a similar 3-day workshop for library faculty and staff, as well as selected faculty from around the campus, and to consult with us on ways in which we might develop collaborations in digital storytelling across the university.

THE CHALLENGE OF MAKING LOTS OF DIGITAL STORIES

While the task of learning to make one digital story is manageable and invigorating, the task of making library digital storytelling programmatic, that is, to attain a critical mass of library stories, is fraught with challenge. There is the challenge of introducing technologies that have traditionally been alien in libraries, and certainly a departure from the technology generally used by library employees. There is the need for administrative support to devote time, training, and equipment to story efforts. There is the challenge of discovering ways to share these stories, which might mean developing appropriate web-based solutions, and also means facing image and soundtrack copyright issues that are also a departure for libraries. And there are less tangible challenges, such as convincing people to think deeply about the personal meaning of their work and to then want to share that professional vulnerability widely. And finally, there is the core challenge, that is also the core payoff, and that is to build the community that can support all these needs and move the process forward.

Because library tradition is textually oriented, the systems on which library employees are trained reflect that. While some may be adept at running equipment for viewing multimedia, it is rare that library staff members are in the business of multimedia production, but instead are consumers and distributors of this form of information.

Another hurdle to developing a critical mass of library stories is administrative support. It can take a neophyte 40 or more hours to complete a 3–4-minute story. Beyond this time commitment are training costs, equipment needs, and some commitment or institutionalized effort to share the stories when they are done. Sometimes training and equipment can be handled through partnerships with others on campus rather than library expenditures, but there must be administrative support for these partnerships to develop and blossom.

A commitment to sharing the stories is essential for the whole endeavor to be meaningful, and is not as insignificant as it may sound. Sharing stories can be done in a variety of ways, such as linking them to the library's website, putting them in an institutional repository, or even uploading them to a service like YouTube. However, placing them in any of these web-accessible environments does not guarantee viewership, certainly not by the intended or most wished-for audience. There need to be meaningful environments in which to share stories in order to elicit feedback, reaction, or conversation with users. The environments can be technical (such as plasma screens in library buildings or on our websites) or personal (such as presentations given to classes). But any environment requires some sort of support—be it server space, equipment, or awareness.

Also of concern when considering how to share digital stories are copyright issues. In the heat of the story-making process it is easy to grab an appropriate picture off the web, or take a song from a CD in one's personal collection, knowing it fits the exact mood that one wishes to convey in the story. Such material needs explicit permissions for use, especially if it is to be shared in a networked environment. Creative Commons licensing helps when available, but often the storyteller needs to acquire permission from the copyright holder or find an alternate recording or image. An image bank of usable pictures or original music clips might be another administrative support that would help storytellers.

Perhaps one of the greatest challenges facing a library wishing to develop a program of digital storytelling is convincing people to go through all the required effort and introspection to tell stories about their professional lives, and then to do so in a way that connects with an audience. In our experience, the greatest motivator is showing examples of others' stories. We have seen these digital story presentations inspire people to look within and often to suddenly realize they do have an interesting story to tell about their own work. But to show examples, a cluster of stories have to be created first; and to get that cluster made, there needs to be either administrative or community support (or both) to begin the process. This in itself is a big step. The second part of this challenge needs to also be highlighted here: even if library staff agree to tell their stories and spend time making something wonderful, if the stories do not engage an audience outside of the library's own staff, the effort might not be worthwhile. Perhaps such stories could be useful for organizational development, but they might not be useful for outreach and engagement of the user community.

This leads finally to the lynchpin challenge, and that is creating a community in which digital storytelling can flourish. This community is represented first by the story circle that ensures that stories are created that can engage the wider community. The story circle provides a safe environment in which storytellers can test the waters of their stories, finding the courage first to be vulnerable in front of this small group before sharing their stories more widely. This means creating a diversity of interest within the story circle so storytellers can know what resonates widely in their stories. The community also needs to have the technical abilities to train, problem-solve, and produce the stories in sharable formats (such as CD, DVD, or streaming media). This community in turn needs to benefit from the shared experience so that the effort invested is worthwhile and valuable to all the participants.

At a recent conference we saw a wonderful digital story that had been created by a 16-year-old girl in response to her mother's seemingly unreachable expectations for her. The girl had made the movie completely on her own and, luckily for the conference attendees, John Seely Brown, the keynote speaker, had happened upon it somewhere. So, a story can be made in isolation. To borrow from the oft-quoted phrase, however, it takes a village to make digital storytelling programmatic. If this girl's story had never made it beyond herself and her mother, it could very well have served a valuable purpose. But, library stories will mean little if they are not shared more widely.

Our own experience with trying to make digital storytelling programmatic is an unfinished story itself. We started by traveling to one of Joe Lambert's workshops. We brought back one story that we shared with several dozen members of the library, other campus faculty, and the university's academic computing department. Our next step was to bring Joe Lambert to our campus to create several stories that could be shared more widely with the campus. We presented these stories in a showcase attended by several dozen more people, and some combination of these stories have been shown in numerous other campus meetings and conference presentations by a variety of the people who participated in that workshop. We have piqued the interest of key people and have encountered much goodwill toward the concept, but regular and continued production of stories remains a work in progress.

THE LIBRARY AND COMMUNITY

Digital stories can help us expose and tap into the deeper human needs that libraries traditionally have helped society address. Chief among these needs is the need for community. Consider how public libraries have supported the needs of and contributed to the meaning of community. They have educated immigrants, fed the imagination of youth, and helped the public to be more enlightened consumers. Through "One Book," branch libraries in public schools, and similar programs, public libraries now are extending their reach beyond just the users who come through their doors to develop the whole community's sense of itself.

Academic libraries are spaces for informal, nonclassroom learning. People learn by reading or talking over a cup of coffee, so coffee bars have entered library buildings. Students find information better when comparing strategies and brainstorming together, so the walls of study carrels have come down and tables with space for more than one person around a computer workstation have replaced them. Learning is social, showing that community is essential to learning. Libraries aren't quiet anymore.

Community is both externally and internally directed. Externally, libraries consider relationships with users. What do users know that others might wish to learn? What happens to a user when he or she interacts with a library's collections? What does he or she care about? Who does he or she become? Increasingly, library users don't necessarily come in to library buildings, but instead just use library services from a distance. Who are they? Do they know who we in the libraries are? Is a library just a bunch of bits and bytes, or do people still work there? If so, who are these people? What exactly do they do? Why do people work in libraries? Answers to these questions help users know what to expect from the library and help the library know what they need. This sort of understanding is essential to directing library evolution and growth.

Libraries need community for ongoing support, as well. All libraries need to develop relationships not only with constituents who use that system's services but also with those who can contribute to its goals. In our increasingly "Googlized" society, the role of the library is no longer taken for granted. Taxpayers may need to know why it is worth upping the funding for their local library. Campus administrators may need a rationale for investing in library buildings along with wireless access to services. Donor relationships rarely happen on a whim. They are cultivated through years of good stewardship, personal encounters, and reputation.

Digital stories can contribute to all these relationships. They can bring public library "One Book" programs to life and enhance the social environment of academic libraries. Digital stories can help us answer questions about the library and its staff for our users, and—when created by our users—can answer our questions about them, too. Digital stories can help donors get to know a curator and let them hear how learners are interacting with other items in a collection. Stories now can allow prospective students into the world of a special collection to learn about the lives behind the artifacts, the photos, the letters, and manuscripts.

Internally, libraries are also organizations in need of community. One academic librarian bemoans the specialization and splintering that has occurred in our large institutions and has made us strangers to our colleagues (Smith 2003, 166). We fester and fight for our own pieces of the pie, resenting what our colleagues get instead of us, rather than seeing our institutions as whole and each person's expertise, talent, and effort as valuable parts of the entire and complex organization. Stories can unify by clarifying the diversity. Stories can remind us of what the other person is doing that is different from what we are doing and how much richer the organization is for that very reason.

Even in business the necessity for using story to build community is becoming apparent. John Seely Brown and his coauthors note the importance of the use of story for problem-solving and development within organizations. When organizations face developmental problems, Brown et al. (2005) note, "[t]hese two elements—the context and the moral [or point]—enable you to apply the story to a new situation, and sometimes many new situations" (65). Stories in organizations can provide direction for a way to develop or insights into how to solve problems. Building community internally as well as externally is important to the health, growth, and the direction of our organizations.

Library digital stories might not be the panacea for every challenge libraries face, but they can become another piece in the tapestry of exploiting emerging technologies to develop new relationships, new services, and new roles for libraries in society. Creating library digital stories presents a number of challenges. Who will tell these stories? How will the storytellers find the supportive environment needed in which to tell them? How will they share their stories? It will only happen with deliberate action.

REFERENCES

Brown, John Seely, Stephen Denning, Katalina Groh, and Laurence Prusak. *Storytelling in Organizations: Why Storytelling is Transforming 21st Century Organizations and Management.* Oxford, UK: Elsevier, 2005.

Lambert, Joe. *Digital Storytelling: Capturing Lives, Creating Community.* Berkeley, CA: Digital Diner Press, 2002.

Pink, Daniel. *A Whole New Mind: Moving from the Information Age to the Conceptual Age.* New York: Riverhead Books, 2005.

Pinker, Steven and Rebecca Goldstein. "Online Interview." *Seed Salon*, no. 2 (May 19, 2004). http://www.seedmagazine.com.

Smith, Kerry, "On Specialization," in *Musings, Meanderings and Monsters Too: Essays on Academic Librarianship*, ed. Martin Raish. Lanham, MD: Scarecrow Press, 2003, pp.166–171.

WEBSITES OF INTEREST

Center for Digital Storytelling
http://www.storycenter.org/
Educational Uses of Digital Storytelling (University of Houston)
http://www.coe.uh.edu/digital-storytelling/
YouTube
http://www.youtube.com

SUGGESTED READINGS

The articles listed below are recommended background reading on some of the topics discussed in this book. Further readings are listed at the end of the individual chapters. Library 2.0 is a new and fast-changing topic area and it's important to note that much of the current discussion is to be found in blogs. Some to check out are ALA TechSource http://www. techsource.ala.org/blog/, LibraryCrunch http://www.librarycrunch.com/, Tame the Web: Libraries and Technology http://tametheweb.com/, and the Shifted Librarian http://www. theshiftedlibrarian.com/.

WEB 2.0 AND LIBRARY 2.0

O'Reilly, Tim. *What is Web 2.0: Design Patterns and Business Models for the Next Generation of Software*, 2005. http://www.oreillynet.com/lpt/a/6228 (accessed May 9, 2006).

More or less the paper that launched a thousand articles, O'Reilly sets the basis for conversation on the concept of Web 2.0. What are the principles that make something Web 2.0? Serving "the long tail," emphasizing services over packaged products, maximizing user participation to both build and enrich services and content, reducing the barriers of intellectual property rights and programming models, and continuous improvement.

Anderson, Chris. "The Long Tail." *Wired*, no. 12.10 (October 2004). http://www.wired. com/wired/archive/12.10/tail.html (accessed December 12, 2006).

Describes the advantages of reaching niche markets. Much Library 2.0 discussion references this article and the concept of serving a large number of people's very individual needs.

Miller, Paul. "Web 2.0: Building the New Library." *Ariadne* 45 (October 2005). http://www. ariadne.ac.uk/issue45/miller/ (accessed October 26, 2006).

Miller outlines eleven principles of Web 2.0 in this brief article: freeing of data, building of virtual applications, participation, works for the user, modular applications, sharing, communication and community building, remixing, smart applications, the Long Tail, and trust. Libraries are encouraged to adapt to these principles.

Chad, Ken and Paul Miller. *Do Libraries Matter? The Rise of Library 2.0.* Talis, November 2005. http://www.talis.com/downloads/white_papers/DoLibrariesMatter.pdf (accessed December 6, 2006).

Building upon the principles outlined in the previous article Talis, a UK-based library products and services company, personnel emphasize the need for libraries to adopt the principles of Web 2.0. These include making the library pervasive on the web, minimizing barriers to use, encouraging the participation of users and other partners, and displacing the integrated library system with modular components that adhere to open standards.

Miller, Paul. "Coming Together around Library 2.0: A Focus for Discussion and a Call to Arms." *D-Lib Magazine* 12, no. 4 (April 2006). http://www.dlib.org/dlib/april06/miller/04miller.html (accessed August 30, 2006).

Further discussion from Talis of the library's need to embrace Web 2.0 concepts. Argues that libraries should stop trying to make users come into the library or to make the library website a destination. Instead, libraries should seek to provide their services as one of many alternatives considered by informed users.

Notess, Greg. "The Terrible Twos: Web 2.0, Library 2.0, and More." *Online* 30, no. 3 (May/June 2006): 40–42.

A brief, understandable explanation of Web 2.0 and library applications. Simple definitions of Ajax, Application Programming Interfaces (APIs), the Long Tail, and tag clouds.

Stephens, Michael. "Web 2.0 & Libraries: Best Practices for Social Software." *Library Technology Reports* 42, no. 4 (July/August 2006).

This entire issue is devoted to a discussion of social web applications and their use in libraries. A good overview of blogs, podcasts, RSS, wikis, instant messaging, and Flickr is provided along with actual examples of library use. Especially recommended is the section on using RSS feeds to make library content available to patrons.

Casey, Michael E. and Laura C. Savastinuk. "Library 2.0." *Library Journal* (September 1, 2006): 40–42.

A brief discussion of ways to begin implementing Web 2.0 into the library, focusing on user-centered change.

Maness, Jack M. "Library 2.0 Theory: Web 2.0 and Its Implications for Libraries." *Webology* 3, no. 2 (June 2006). http://www.webology.ir/2006/v3n2/a25.html (accessed August 1, 2006).

An attempt to define and theorize on the nature of Library 2.0. Maness provides four essential elements: user-centered, multimedia, socially rich, and communally innovative. The article goes on to discuss synchronous messaging, streaming media, blogs and wikis, social networks, tagging, RSS, and mashups and their uses in libraries.

CATALOG 2.0

Antelman, Kristin, Emily Lynema, and Andrew K. Pace. "Toward a Twenty-First Century Library Catalog." *Information Technology and Libraries* 25 (September 2006): 128–139.

A detailed discussion of North Carolina State University's implementation of Endeca's Information Access Platform to provide relevance-ranked keyword searching, enhanced browsing, spell-checking, and improved controlled subject access from the library catalog.

Bisson, Casey. "Designing an OPAC for Web 2.0." Presentation at the 2006 Mid-Atlantic Innovative Users Group, Philadelphia, October 27, 2006. http://maisonbisson.com/blog/post/11483/.

This is a set of slides of Bisson's presentation about incorporating Web 2.0 software into the library catalog. Bisson has developed a WordPress (a blog application) OPAC at Plymouth State University.

Blyberg, John. "Catalog Annotations." *Library Journal* 131 (September 1, 2006): 32.

A whimsical example of using social software in library catalogs. Blyberg's program lets users generate an old-fashioned looking card catalog, create or read others' annotations, and build a personal catalog collection.

Wilder, Stanley. "Baker's Smudges." *Library Journal* 131 (September 1, 2006): 30–32.

What is the electronic equivalent to dirt smudges on catalog cards as indicators of quality based on high use? Wilder briefly discusses the need for library catalogs to incorporate more user-created information.

DIGITAL STORYTELLING

Lambert, Joe. *Digital Storytelling: Capturing Lives, Creating Community.* Berkeley, CA: Digital Diner Press, 2002.

GAMING

Levine, Jenny. "Gaming & Libraries: Intersection of Services." *Library Technology Reports* 42, no. 5 (September/October 2006).

Levine delves into the philosophical issues surrounding gaming in libraries, making a case for games as promotional tools to encourage users, especially boys, to come to the library as well as the benefits of gaming for cognitive and social development. She is specific about what to buy and how to set it up and provides examples of gaming in use in school, public, and academic libraries.

HANDHELD COMPUTERS

Cuddy, Colleen. "How to Serve Content to PDA Users On-the-Go." *Computers in Libraries* 26 (April 2006): 10–15.

Tips on making your library's website usable for PDA viewing.

MASHUPS AND WEB SERVICES

Breeding, Marshall. "Web Services and the Service-Oriented Architecture." *Library Technology Reports* 42, no. 3 (May/June 2006).

Breeding describes web services as "fancy plumbing for the Web," which is apt as it turns out web services are not what a non-IT librarian might think they are but are very important to know about.

PODCASTING

Worcester, Lea and Evelyn Barker. "Podcasting: Exploring the Possibilities for Academic Libraries." *College & Undergraduate Libraries* 13, no. 3 (2006): 87–91.

Colombo, George W. and Curtis Franklin, Jr. *Absolute Beginner's Guide to Podcasting*. Indianapolis: Que, 2006.

SOCIAL BOOKMARKING

Gordon-Murnane, Laura. "Social Bookmarking, Folksonomies, and Web 2.0 Tools." *Searcher* 14 (June 2006): 26–38.

Dye, Jessica. "Folksonomy: A Game of High-Tech (and High-Stakes) Tag." *EContent* 29 (April 2006): 38–43.

This doesn't address libraries but is a good overall discussion of social tagging and its uses in Internet searching.

SOCIAL NETWORKING

Evans, Beth. "Your Space or MySpace." *Library Journal* 131 (October 15, 2006): 8–12.

Advice for academic libraries on creating a presence in MySpace. Includes links to some other libraries' (including public) MySpace profiles.

WIKIS

Chawner, Brenda and Paul H. Lewis. "WikiWikiWebs: New Ways to Communicate in a Web Environment." *Information Technology and Libraries* 25 (March 2006): 33–43.

A detailed discussion of wikis, including history and development, features, choosing wiki software, and examples of use in library and information management.

See also Michael Stephens' section on wikis in *Library Technology Reports* noted above under Web 2.0 and Library 2.0.

INDEX

ABOUT THE EDITOR
AND CONTRIBUTORS

LORI BELL is Director of Innovation for the Alliance Library System and has been involved in the setup and implementation of the Alliance Second Life Library. She has worked in a variety of library settings and was named a *Library Journal* "Mover and Shaker" in 2004.

STEVEN J. BELL is Associate University Librarian for Research and Instructional Services at Temple University. Prior to that he was Director of the Paul J. Gutman Library at Philadelphia University and Assistant Director at the Wharton School at the University of Pennsylvania, where he also earned his Ed.D. in 1997. He writes and speaks frequently on topics such as information retrieval, library and learning technologies, and academic librarianship. An Adjunct Professor at the Drexel University College of Information Science and Technology, he teaches courses in online searching, academic librarianship, and business information resources. He maintains a website and weblog, "Steven Bell's Keeping Up Web Site" and "The Kept-Up Academic Librarian," that promote current awareness skills and resources. Steven is a cofounder of the Blended Librarian's Online Learning Community on the Learning Times Network and has participated in numerous virtual presentations. For additional information about Steven J. Bell or to find links to the various websites he publishes and maintains, point your browser to http://stevenbell.info.

ELIZABETH L. BLACK is a Systems Librarian and Assistant Professor at The Ohio State University Libraries. Her primary responsibilities include the institutional repository, Knowledge Bank, and the Libraries website. She is involved in several projects to implement Web 2.0 tools at OSU Libraries. Elizabeth also worked for 13 years at the Columbus Metropolitan Library in a variety of jobs involving technology and customer service. Elizabeth received her Masters of Library Science from Kent State University in Kent, Ohio, and a B.A. and a B.S. from Miami University, Oxford, Ohio.

CHAD F. BOENINGER is a Reference and Instruction Librarian at Ohio University's Alden Library. He is also the Business and Economics Bibliographer and the assistant web manager. Chad began working at Ohio University in July 2002, shortly after receiving his Master of Science in Information Sciences from the University of Tennessee. Chad's research interests include multiple aspects of technology, library marketing, library planning, library instruction, and public services. He is constantly striving to make the library a cool place and a viable resource for current and future patrons. He is the author of the Library Voice blog.

MICHAEL CASEY is the Division Director of Technology Services for the Gwinnett County Public Library. He recently published an article in Library Journal titled "Library 2.0: Service for the Next-Generation Library." His book, also on Library 2.0, is due to be published by Information Today Press in early 2007. He is also the author of the blog LibraryCrunch. Michael has an M.L.S. from Southern Connecticut State, an M.A. in Political Science from Penn State, and a B.A. from Duquesne University. He lives just outside of Atlanta with his wife and two kids.

NANCY COURTNEY is Coordinator of Outreach and Learning at the Ohio State University Libraries and the editor of *Technology for the Rest of Us: A Primer on Computer Technologies for the Low-Tech Librarian* (Libraries Unlimited, 2005). She has a B.A. in Classics from Northwestern University and an M.S. in Library and Information Science from the University of Illinois.

KAREN DIAZ is an Instruction Librarian at the Ohio State University Libraries. She teaches and develops courses and instructional programs for college level research skills, with a special interest in distance and online learning. Karen holds an M.L.I.S. from Louisiana State University. Her research interests include online reference and research, and digital storytelling in libraries.

ANNE M. FIELDS is Coordinator for Research and Reference and Subject Specialist for English at The Ohio State University Libraries. She holds a B.A. from Mount Holyoke College, an M.A. in Library Science from the University of Iowa, and a Ph.D. in English from the University of North Carolina-Chapel Hill. She has worked in libraries ranging from high school to community college to small college and large research universities. Her research interests include cognition as it relates to information-seeking and use, how the politics of academic disciplines are reflected in library resources and organizational structures, and digital storytelling in libraries.

CHRIS KRETZ is the Digital Resources Librarian at Dowling College, located in Oakdale, New York. He received his Master of Library Science degree from Queens College, City University of New York, and a Master of Arts in Liberal Studies degree from Stony Brook University. He is project manager for the Historic Oakdale digital collection and creator of the Dowling College Library podcast Omnibus.

ELLYSSA KROSKI is a Reference Librarian for Columbia University as well as an independent Information Consultant and national conference speaker. She has been working with Information and Internet technologies for over 10 years and specializes in Web 2.0 technology. Ellyssa is currently writing a book for Neal-Schuman Publishers about Web 2.0 technologies and libraries. She teaches professional development seminars at a library consortium in New York City and writes a successful blog called InfoTangle. She is a member of an international library honor society, and holds an M. L. I. S. from Long Island University.

BRIAN S. MATHEWS is an Information Services Librarian at the Georgia Institute of Technology. He is the subject liaison for Mechanical Engineering and Computer Science, and is the coordinator for distance learning support services. Brian frequently presents and publishes on the library applications of social web technologies, and chronicles his experiments on his blog The Ubiquitous Librarian (http://theubiquitouslibrarian.typepad.com)

TOM PETERS is the founder of TAP Information Services (www. tapinformation.com), which provides a wide variety of services supporting libraries, library consortia, government agencies, publishers, and other information-intensive organizations. Tom has worked previously at the Committee on Institutional Cooperation (CIC, the academic consortium of the Big Ten universities and the University of Chicago), Western Illinois University in Macomb, Northern Illinois University in DeKalb, Minnesota State University at Mankato, and the University of Missouri at Kansas City. Tom did his undergraduate work at Grinnell College, where he majored in English and philosophy. He earned his library science degree at the University of Iowa. His second master's degree (in English) was completed at the University of Missouri at Kansas City. His library experience includes reference service, library instruction, collection management, and administration. His current interests include library services in virtual worlds, online programming using web conferencing software, and digital audio books.

KITTY POPE is Executive Director of the Alliance Library System and has worked in libraries in several countries, including the most recent, Calgary Public Library. Her interests include building interactive web presences for libraries and innovative efforts to make libraries dynamic for the twenty-first century.

ERIC SCHNELL is an Associate Professor and Head of Information Technology at the Prior Health Sciences Library at The Ohio State University. Holding an M. L. S. from the University at Buffalo, he has spent the last 16 years working in academic medical libraries as a reference librarian, technology facilitator, and as a manager of networked services. He has presented at library conferences locally, nationally, and internationally in the area of technology and libraries and writes on these topics in is blog The Medium is the Message (http://ericschnell.blogspot.com).

In 2005, Schnell was named a *Library Journal* "Mover and Shaker" and has been involved with two projects that have won the Medical Library Association's ISI/Frank Bradway Rogers Information Advancement Award. He was a National Library of Medicine Medical Informatics Fellow (Woods Hole, MA) in 2003. He is an open source advocate and has taught the topic online for The University of North Carolina at Chapel Hill, School of Information and Library Science.

CHRISTOPHER STRAUBER is the Reference & Web Services Librarian at Wofford College in Spartanburg, South Carolina. His M. L.I. S. is from Kent State University, and his M.A. in Ancient History is from the University of Cincinnati. His interests include the Roman army, open source software, the future of research in the humanities, user-centered web design, and other related subjects. His first handheld was a Palm Zire.

DAVID WARD is the Head of Information Services at the University of Illinois Undergraduate Library. He started the library's gaming collection in the spring of 2006, is chair of the library's gaming group, and also organizes gaming nights and other promotional events.

David publishes and presents in the area of chat reference, instant messaging, and electronic reserves. His research interests include the role and application of technology to public services, and the impacts of patron use and adoption of new technologies on libraries.